Kaylien Morrell
(from Margie
Christmas 1961)

Met Mrs Ward, Dec 31,1961, CBR DINNER.

THE CAPSULE
OF THE MIND

THE CAPSULE
OF THE MIND

Chapters in the Life of
Emily Dickinson

THEODORA WARD

THE BELKNAP PRESS OF
HARVARD UNIVERSITY PRESS

Cambridge, Massachusetts

1961

Poems by Emily Dickinson included in this volume are reprinted by permission of the President and Fellows of Harvard College and the Trustees of Amherst College from THE POEMS OF EMILY DICKINSON, edited by Thomas H. Johnson, The Belknap Press of Harvard University Press, Cambridge, Mass., copyright, 1951 and 1955, by the President and Fellows of Harvard College.

Distributed in Great Britain by Oxford University Press, London

Library of Congress Catalog Card Number 61-13746

Printed in the United States of America

PREFACE

Very few figures in the literary scene of recent times have taken such a strong hold on the minds of their readers as that of Emily Dickinson. It is almost impossible to give concentrated attention to her poems and letters without wishing to probe the source from which came the extraordinary power of her poetic utterance. The quality of personal involvement pervades not only the most lyrical of her poems but the most abstract as well, leading the reader to seek farther than an intellectual or aesthetic stimulus for an explanation of their origin. Genius may be wholly spontaneous, but it cannot manifest itself without making use of the elements that comprise the individual it has endowed. It is by following the main stream of the emotional life that we come closest to the creative sources. This small book does not claim to be an analysis of the mind of Emily Dickinson or a consistent account of all that was emotionally significant in her life, but it is offered as a contribution toward a better understanding of the woman who, unknown to herself or her friends, was one of the world's great poets.

The six essays that make up the volume were written at different times, as the various phases of the poet's life took their turn at the center of my attention. Four of them have already been published, at least in part. Some revisions have been made in two of these, to avoid repetition and insure continuity.

The sequence of three studies of phases in Emily Dickinson's emotional life contained in Part One grew out of the impressions I received during seven years of intimate association with her manuscripts, in my work as assistant to Thomas H. Johnson, editor of *The Poems of Emily Dickinson*, (Harvard, 1955), and as associate editor with him of *The Letters of Emily Dickinson*, (Harvard, 1958). To Mr. Johnson I am very grateful for the matchless opportunity he gave me, and for the fellowship enjoyed in the work.

The essay that appears here as the second chapter, "Ourself behind Ourself," was the first of the three to be written. It was the result of my study of the poems for a subject index. As the poems now appear, arranged chronologically by years, the startling fact is revealed that the great bulk of her creative work as a poet was produced between her twenty-ninth and thirty-sixth years, culminating in 1862 with an overwhelming output of three hundred and sixty-six poems. In this arrangement the pattern of content and emotional intensity is revealed, and it becomes inescapably clear that the writer at that time was passing through a severe emotional and psychological crisis. The only known statement in her own words concerning this period in her life is in her second letter to Thomas Wentworth Higginson, when in answer to his questions she said, "I had a terror — since September — I could tell to none – and so I sing, as the boy does by the Burying Ground – because I am afraid." In the period of greatest stress she wrote:

PREFACE

The Martyr Poets – did not tell –
But wrought their Pang in syllable –
That when their mortal name be numb –
Their mortal fate – encourage Some –
The Martyr Painters – never spoke –
Bequeathing – rather – to their Work –
That when their conscious fingers cease –
Some seek in Art – the Art of Peace –

She consciously took the artist's path to peace, and worked her way through deep and agonizing conflict, recording the steps in her poems.

The disturbance was of a spontaneous nature, not the result of any one set of circumstances, but the effect on a sensitive personality of slowly accumulated pressures, both within and without, working against inherent forces for growth and fulfillment. In the ensuing struggle, so painful that it might have wrecked a weaker mind, she preserved her sanity by the transformation into art of all phases of her inner experience during the time of crisis.

An attempt to trace the inner story through the self-revelation to be found in her poems and letters is open to the serious danger of drawing false inferences. When she said

I dwell in Possibility –
A fairer House than Prose –

she was pointing out that all human experience is open for a poet's choice. One must also take note of her warning to Thomas Wentworth Higginson in one of her first letters to him: "When I state myself, as the Representative of the Verse – it does not mean – me – but a supposed person."

However, it may be permissible to assume that she was referring specifically to the small selection from her many verses that she had chosen to send. It is also evident that, whether or not the subject matter of a poem deals with circumstances of time and place, the poet himself speaks through it. He not only shows his conscious attitudes, but inevitably reveals something of his unconscious mind, both on a personal level and on the deeper one that touches his relation to those underlying psychological patterns common to all men.

Among Emily Dickinson's poems few appear to be direct and uncensored expressions of symbols from the unconscious. With an extraordinary awareness she transformed experience into art, in which the images, though spontaneous, are usually related to the conscious sensation or evaluation of the experience instead of being an outpouring from the depths of the psyche. In trying to trace the events in her inner world, then, one must to a large extent follow the experience as she became aware of it, rather than attempt an analysis of the images and symbols according to any preconceived idea of their significance. Some of the poems with which I shall deal are poetically inferior, as is often true when the subject matter is related to an aspect of the writer's mind that is not yet fully realized, or when the verses are written to relieve a tension not clearly understood.

In choosing the poems that seem most indicative of Emily's struggle, I have omitted the poems of nature, those that concern other people, and, for the most part, those that give expression to her conscious wrestling with the problem of death and the fantasies she built around the grave and the life be-

yond it. Regardless of their literary value, I have picked out
those poems written in the first person that show intense emotion and uncontrollable moods, a few that are so unrelated to
reality as to betray their origin in the subconscious world of
dream and phantasm, and those that are connected with the
themes of love and the lover, around which was centered the
main area of her suffering. By following these poems, even in
a sequence that can be only broadly true in time, the scenes
of the inner drama become apparent to a surprising degree.

The first and third chapters are concerned with the conditions that led to the years of crisis and the subsequent development of Emily's inner life. Her letters are the principal
source from which the material was drawn.

The three friendships that are discussed in Part Two are
those that are represented by the largest surviving groups of
letters from Emily Dickinson to persons other than members
of her family. All of these friends were important to her, but
her relations with them were not necessarily the most significant in her life. Since none of the letters she wrote to the
Reverend Charles Wadsworth have been found, and those to
Judge Otis P. Lord exist — so far as is now known — only in
drafts that remained with her own papers, the outline of her
relations with these two men must remain incomplete. The
letters to the Hollands, to Samuel Bowles and his wife, and
to Thomas Wentworth Higginson, however, form a source
not only for an understanding of the friendships they record,
but shed light also on various aspects of her life and of her
relations with others.

The chapter on the Hollands is based largely on the intro-

PREFACE

duction I wrote as editor of *Emily Dickinson's Letters to Dr. and Mrs. Josiah Gilbert Holland*, (Harvard, 1951); it has been revised to include some comments from the body of the book as well as new material. I acknowledge with thanks the cordial permission of Mr. Zoltan Haraszti, editor of the *Boston Public Library Quarterly*, to reprint the article "Emily Dickinson and T. W. Higginson," which was published in that journal for January 1953. "Ourself behind Ourself" and "The Finest Secret" first appeared in the *Harvard Library Bulletin*, in the issues of Winter 1956 and Winter 1960 respectively. My thanks for permission to reprint these articles would not be complete without a word of gratitude to the editor, Mr. G. W. Cottrell, and to other friends who have contributed through their personal interest in the preparation of this book.

CONTENTS

PART ONE

TO LIVE IS ENDOWMENT

A life may be regarded from several angles. It can be seen as a series of events, a record of accomplishment, or, from the subject's own view, it can appear as an accumulation of experience. It may also be observed as the working out of a pattern, not predestined, but evolving surely from within a unique personality. Perceived only dimly, perhaps, in the living, the pattern takes shape as outer circumstances allow and inner powers govern the choice of alternatives. There are many phases to pass through as it unfolds, each one having its effect on the one to come. These three chapters attempt to follow the continuing movement of the spirit through some of the phases in the life of Emily Dickinson.

MY DELINQUENT PALACES

Elements in the inner life
of the young Emily Dickinson

In 1840, when Emily Dickinson was nine years old, a young painter named Otis Bullard, attempting to pay off the debts incurred in his education, spent some weeks in Amherst and took likenesses of a number of important persons in the town. At the home of Edward Dickinson he painted the entire family — the father and mother each separately, the children in a group. The bodies of the children, undersized and stiff in formal clothes, like images modeled in clay, give the impression that the artist prepared them in advance, or worked them up at home after he had completed the heads from life. The faces, however, are real and animated, and, in spite of a tendency to uniformity in the noses and the strongly set lips of all three, definite personalities appear on the canvas. The face of the future poet expresses already the quality of awareness that was to be a major component of her mind, the eyes serious, yet ready to respond to any suggestion of hilarity. Avoiding the problems involved in painting hands, the artist suggested their presence by placing objects in their grasp to hide them. Whether or not the choice was fortuitous,

3

he succeeded in furnishing Emily and Lavinia with properties that remained characteristic throughout their lives. In Lavinia's lap is a picture of a cat, and in Emily's hand lies a moss rose on an open book, where a drawing of the same flower is shown.

It would not have been in accord with Edward Dickinson's nature to commission portraits of any of his family without including them all. The solidarity of the family group fitted well in that time and place, for the community was made up of self-sustaining homes in which the inhabitants were highly organized social units. At that time, Amherst's village green was still a rough pasture with birch trees and a frog pond, and the houses around it and along the few roads that led away from it were modified farms, provided with horses, cows, and chickens, vegetable gardens and orchards. Water was drawn by hand or by means of a pump from a well near the house. Many families owned their own woodlots, where the fuel was cut to supply their stoves and open hearths. No street lights brightened the paths along the unpaved roads. At night each house became a little island, where indoors the family gathered around an oil lamp after dark, and went to bed by the light of a tallow candle, which made wavering shadows where familiar objects had been. When Emily reminded her school friend Jane Humphrey, in one of her earliest letters, how they had enjoyed jumping into bed when they slept together, she was doubtless recalling a moment of genuine adventure, in which, after the tiny flame was extinguished, total blackness enveloped the room as the two little girls plunged together into the middle of a billowing feather bed.

MY DELINQUENT PALACES

Emily's tie to her home was fundamental and strong, and was never broken, though her personal life within its frame was destined to undergo an inner revolution. As a child she lived in a close atmosphere of parental solicitude, presided over by a devoted father who was the figure of security and authority. How far he carried his responsibility into the management of affairs in his home is shown in his letters to his wife during the seasons when his political interests took him to Boston. "Must" and "must not" appear often, not only in the messages to the children, but in his admonitions to their mother. His attitude is not that of a dictator demanding his will, but an anxious husband and father delegating responsibility for the welfare of his family. The hired girl and Austin, then about seven, were to carry the water from the well in the barnyard. To his wife he said, *"You must not go into the yard yourself,* on any account — there is no necessity for it and you *must not do it."* She must not be afraid at night, but call on Divine Providence for support. The children must be very careful about taking cold, in this pleasant weather, and Lavinia, particularly, must be closely watched, to guard against croup. To Emily he said, when she was seven, "You must not go to school when it is cold or bad going — You must be very careful & not get sick."

Rectitude was kept ever before the children's minds, often with the promise of a reward. Their father's whole ambition for them was summed up in one letter, where he wrote, "I want to have you grow up, & become good men and women — and learn all you can, so that you can teach others to do right." Responsibility for themselves and others was enjoined

5

from their earliest years. To Austin at eight he wrote, "Get in your wood — help Catharine get the water — and if the barn well gets so low that you can't get any, you must ask Mr. Mack if he will let you get it out of his house well — If you & Catharine can't get it, you must get Daniel Barnard to help you, & I will pay him." Austin's response to this charge is not recorded, but it is probable that his duties had not then aged him prematurely, since his father added in the next sentence, "You must be good at the table."

However possessive and dictatorial Edward Dickinson's love for his family may have seemed, it was a genuine emotion, with a hidden warmth that rarely expressed itself. While he was away from home his constant longing to be with his wife and children appeared in every letter; yet it is probable that when he was once in the midst of the "domestic felicity" for which he yearned, the children saw little of the deep tenderness that underlay his anxiety for their health and safety, and his desire for their moral advancement. He never entered their world, only stooping occasionally to what he believed was their level, to bring them presents and rewards for good behavior. It was an adult world of stern fact to which he introduced them, and their happiness depended on how they adapted themselves to it. He did not wish to keep them from play — he had his own pleasure in driving the fastest horse in town — but play served no end in itself, and was secondary to the duties each human being was called upon to perform.

The children felt themselves to be a part of the community, where everyone was known and ties were so interwoven that anyone's concern was the concern of all. News and gossip were distinguishable only by the motives that lay behind them. Emily, at eleven, writing to Austin, who was away at school, knew that her brother would be as interested in hearing that Mr. Jones's insurance turned out to be eight thousand instead of six thousand as he would be in her account of the attacks made on his pet rooster by its fellows. Edward Dickinson, coming home from the office in his tall hat, brought legal language to the dinner table, spiced with reports heard along the way of the latest events in town. The habit that grew up among the Dickinson children of lampooning their neighbors may have had its origin in the characterizations formed by their father's keen and critical mind. Through their mother they were more directly connected with the joys and the calamities in the families of Amherst, rich and poor. Death hung like a thundercloud over every household, regardless of economic status, and required not only the sympathy but the ministrations of those who lived near. To talk of all these things was an accepted part of the children's lives. Out of it grew Emily's understanding of human suffering.

There was little encouragement for fantasy in the mental atmosphere of Amherst in the eighteen thirties and forties. The imagination was directed to the embellishment of life rather than to pure invention for its own sake. Sentimental ballads poured from the pens of rural versifiers, and comic relief was found in tall tales and mock heroics. The young people expanded St. Valentine's Day into a season for the free exchange of effusions, often using considerable ingenuity in their parodies of the romantic style.

7

The children probably had access to *The Arabian Nights*, and knew some of the old-world folk tales, such as "Cinderella" and "Jack the Giant Killer," but indulgence in such fantastic literature was somewhat frowned upon. The wealth of fairy tales that brought delight to the next generation of American children, after the work of the Grimm brothers and the stories of Hans Christian Andersen had made their great contributions, had not yet flowed into the stream of popular literature. For the children of Amherst in the eighteen forties the fields and woods were not peopled with elves and fairies. These had been left behind in England by the ancestors, two centuries earlier. The only magical beings Emily had to count on were the angels, as she met them in the Bible and the hymn book.

The human world of her parents was matched by another world above, real but invisible, where God alone ruled as her father ruled in her earthly home. The angels who lived there were endowed with human characteristics, and their life was based on the family pattern:

> God permits industrious Angels –
> Afternoons – to play –

is an image that could not have originated in the mind of the woman of thirty Emily was when she wrote it, but was certainly carried over from the impressions of childhood. The frequency with which angels appear in Emily's earlier poems suggests that their bright presences had often been invoked when she was a child as a means of escape from the dullness of routine. A poem in light vein, written in protest against science as the great destroyer of illusion, deplores the loss of the old-fashioned Heaven with such vehemence that the strength of her early attachment to it is revealed. In the fifth stanza of "Arcturus is his other name," she complains,

> What once was "Heaven"
> Is *"Zenith"* now –
> Where I proposed to go
> When Time's brief masquerade was done
> Is mapped and charted too.

In the final stanzas she reverts completely to the little girl attitude, refusing for the moment to give up the hope of security in the Heaven of "the Father in the skies."

In spite of excursions into Heaven, Emily seems to have found that it was the earth itself that held her most enthralled, when her sensitive awareness led her out, little by little, beyond the infant realm. The forces of nature controlled much of the life in her own home and that of the village. Cold, heat, floods, and drought all had an immediate effect on everyday living. Emily must have received ineradicable impressions from such experiences as being overtaken by a severe thunderstorm in an open carriage when she was two and a half years old. Her young aunt, Lavinia Norcross, with whom she was traveling to Monson to visit her mother's family, recounted in a letter to Mrs. Dickinson that Emily had not cried, though she soberly asked to be taken to her mother when she saw the fearful flashes of "fire" in the sky. In her aunt's arms, her face covered by the loose cloak that enveloped them both, she silently endured what was probably her first experience of awe. The occasion may have been forgotten, but the lasting effect appears in the recurrence in her poems of the theme of the storm, with its threat of dissolution to the frail works of man.

Nothing escaped her observation. The natural world met her on the doorstep, and the sounds of it were present even in her own room. She could not escape the claims of the earth, where daily miracles of seed and flower took place, or of the air with its ceaseless motion and its freight of ever-changing clouds. Her letters to Abiah Root, beginning when she was fourteen, full as they are of schoolgirl chatter, show that living was carried on in full consciousness of the daily phases of nature. She could not have been more than ten years old when, during a school term, she shared her room with a pupil from another town, yet a dozen years later she recalled in a letter to Jane Humphrey the delight of sitting with her in the doorway after school, watching the birds in the cherry trees beside the house. What the children talked of had long been forgotten, but the distant sound of an axe in the woods remained in Emily's memory as a part of the setting, adding spaciousness to the intimacy of their companionship.

Going to school was to Emily, as to many children of her day, a privilege to be seized and acted upon with full enjoyment. The Amherst Academy had four terms a year, but few pupils attended for more than two, and the classes were ungraded. In Emily's case there was the danger that at any moment her parents might decide to withdraw her on account of her health, as actually happened more than once. School not only meant the joy of acquiring knowledge, but the stimulation of contact with alert and informed minds. Most of her teachers were well educated young people in their twenties, just old enough to excite her admiration and young enough to be approachable. They formed a natural link for her with a larger world of the mind. The companionship of girls of her own age gave her an outlet not only for her strong affections, but for the spontaneous flow of fanciful expression that comes from the mere joy of living. She was especially attracted to Abiah Root because, on the day when the girls first met at school, Abiah had decorated herself with green curls made of the stems of dandelions.

In view of these evidences of her full participation in the life around her, it is surprising to read a poem written twenty years later, as she reviewed the path by which she had come. She looks back upon herself as a child who already recognized an aspect of life that she could not share with those around her.

> It would have starved a Gnat –
> To live so small as I –
> And yet I was a living Child –
> With Food's necessity
>
> Upon me – like a Claw –
> I could no more remove
> Than I could coax a Leech away –
> Or make a Dragon – move –
>
> Nor like the Gnat – had I –
> The privilege to fly
> And seek a Dinner for myself –
> How mightier He – than I –
>
> Nor like Himself – the Art
> Upon the Window Pane

TO LIVE IS ENDOWMENT

To gad my little Being out –
And not begin – again –

The famine of the spirit pictured here makes one wonder why Emily did not seek escape from her environment as the Brontë sisters did, by writing elaborate tales of a world of their own. If she ever did, no evidence has remained among her papers. The answer seems to lie in the difference between the nature of her loneliness and that of the "the Yorkshire Girls" whom she so greatly admired. There was no physical hardship in the Dickinsons' way of living. Emily's environment was less isolated and of warmer tones than that of the parsonage at Haworth. She grew up in a town where there was plenty of mental stimulus and an unusual number of people of distinction. She was privileged to attend a school that was formed by the demands of the community itself, and where teaching of subjects took precedence over mere training. She had such a strong hold on reality through her closeness to nature in Amherst's gentle landscape, the companionship of a chosen group of schoolmates, and a sense of participation in the life of the community, that she did not need to project herself into an imaginary setting.

Emily's hunger was for a missing element — something deeply felt but unknown — that, in spite of all the world offered, gripped her "like a Claw." What she needed was a way to alleviate the spiritual loneliness of carrying a burden she did not understand. Called into existence to meet this particular need, she seems to have had, as many children do at five or six years, an imaginary companion. Usually a child who projects a part of himself into a separate personality pictures the companion as of the same sex, but Emily's alter ego seems to have been a boy named Tim. In a curious poem, written in childlike language at a time when her creative flood was reaching its height, she unexpectedly returned to the mood of a lonely child, burdened with a secret fear she could not bear alone. About 1860 she wrote:

> We dont cry – Tim and I,
> We are far too grand –
> But we bolt the door tight
> To prevent a friend –
>
> Then we hide our brave face
> Deep in our hand –
> Not to cry – Tim and I –
> We are far too grand –
>
> Nor to dream – he and me –
> Do we condescend –
> We just shut our brown eye
> To see to the end –
>
> Tim – see Cottages –
> But, Oh, so high!
> Then – we shake – Tim and I –
> And lest I – cry –
>
> Tim – reads a little Hymn –
> And we both pray –
> Please, Sir, I and Tim –
> Always lost the way!
>
> We must die – by and by –
> Clergyman say –
> Tim – shall – if I – do –
> I – too – if he –

TO LIVE IS ENDOWMENT

How shall we arrange it –
Tim – was – so – shy?
Take us simultaneous – Lord –
I – "Tim" – and – Me!

Tim's little figure seems still alive in her memory as she writes of how he shares the terror that has driven her into solitude. Her shy masculine counterpart offers no help except when he "reads a little Hymn" — an act that is prophetic of his true function as the part of her that is to become a poet. The terror seems to be concerned with getting lost, presumably in the search for Heaven, and it is characteristic of Emily's mind that her way of dealing with her trouble is neither through tears nor by dreaming, but with the effort "To see to the end." What she sees is a cozy heaven, with "Cottages – But, Oh, so high!" — a conception she was to play with later in such poems as "I went to Heaven – 'Twas a small Town," yet the fear persists that she and her inner companion might be separated by death. Tim was so important to her that he must not be lost, and indeed he was to reappear in different guises, later in her life.

The spiritual hunger that led her into the search for Heaven was given a more specific delineation in another poem written a few years later.

A loss of something ever felt I –
The first that I could recollect
Bereft I was – of what I knew not
Too young that any should suspect

A Mourner walked among the children
I notwithstanding went about

MY DELINQUENT PALACES

As one bemoaning a Dominion
Itself the only Prince cast out –

Elder, Today, a session wiser
And fainter, too, as Wiseness is –
I find myself still softly searching
For my Delinquent Palaces –

And a Suspicion, like a Finger
Touches my Forehead now and then
That I am looking oppositely
For the site of the Kingdom of Heaven –

"Intimations of immortality" were to Emily, as to other children destined to be artists, not present glory, as Wordsworth supposes, but the suffering of separateness. She came to feel that her own nature was intended for some other and richer destiny than she could find in the way of life and the patterns of thought of the people who surrounded her. What she sought was not something wholly apart from the world she knew, but a new dimension within it, of which others were so unaware that they apparently did not feel the lack of it.

While these first stirrings of an inner search were making themselves felt during Emily's adolescence, she was subjected to a form of collective pressure commonly experienced by her contemporaries and found herself faced with the demands of her social group for an open acceptance of the Christian faith as it was interpreted by the churches of her time. She was thrown into a grave conflict. This was one way to find Heaven, but from the beginning she was unable to fit herself into the pattern that was required.

It was an age of religious revivals, which seemed to arise spontaneously and were considered the direct intervention of

God and a sign of his favor. Amherst College, which was founded to promote an evangelical Christian culture, and most of whose professors were ministers, was periodically subject to such seasons of religious agitation. Professor Edward Hitchcock, who taught chemistry and geology in the college for nearly forty years and served as its president for part of that time, recalled that there had been twelve important revivals while he was connected with the college. His predecessor as president, the Reverend Heman Humphrey, professor of theology, moral philosophy, and metaphysics, believed so firmly in the value of revivals that he wrote two books to be used as manuals by ministers conducting them. The pattern they set must have brought terror to many a young heart. Although Emily may never have had direct contact with Dr. Humphrey, the atmosphere that emanated from him in the little town, of which the college was an integral part, is reflected in a letter she wrote to Mrs. Holland seven years after the time of her adolescent struggle. Acknowledging that the joy she felt when she thought of her new friend had led her into irresponsible behavior, she said, "Monday, I solemnly resolved I would be *sensible,* so I wore thick shoes, and thought of Dr. Humphrey and the Moral Law."

In his little book *Revival Conversations,* published in 1844, Dr. Humphrey demonstrated how to lead an inquirer into a state of repentance. A young man, troubled by his failure to be touched by the appeals he sees others responding to, comes to ask what steps he must take to find the religious experience that is expected of him. The minister asks him whether he has repented and given his heart to God.

INQUIRER   O, you misunderstand me. I have not got so far. I have told you already that I am not even awakened yet, and how can I repent? I am somewhat troubled, to be sure, or I should not be here. But my feelings are all indefinite.

PASTOR   Do you think your not having *got so far* is any valid excuse for not repenting, and giving your heart to God? The question is not, how far you have advanced, but how far you *ought* to have advanced, — not how you feel, but how you *ought* to feel.

INQUIRER   I do not feel anything. I have no sense of my sins, and how can I have? I wish I could feel as others do, but it is impossible.

PASTOR   My dear young friend, do stop and think what you are saying. You do not feel! You have no sense of sinfulness! Astonishing! A sinner against a holy God, and under condemnation, and liable every moment to drop into a burning hopeless eternity — and yet cannot feel, cannot be alarmed, cannot "flee from the wrath to come." O, how stupid you must be!

The stages that led to conversion appear, according to the testimony of those who took part in the revivals, to have occurred in a recognized order. First there was a state of alarm, brought on by the preaching or persuasion of friends. Seeing the happiness of those who have surrendered, the person envied them their peace of mind. Then came a period of increasing conflict, ending in a conviction of sin that often brought severe depression. At the moment of highest tension, sometimes of despair, there came a release, a letting go, followed by a tranquilizing flood of comfort in the sense of the presence of God. At last the whole being was filled with joy and a desire to praise the Lord, who had shown such mercy.

Not only in revival times were the young people subjected

to the demand for repentance since the same theme reached them from the pulpits of the churches they attended every Sunday. In the awakening period of adolescence, conversion was looked for by solicitous elders and applauded by contemporaries who had already passed through its throes. To become a practicing Christian was in a sense analagous to the initiation rites of primitive peoples, by which the adolescent becomes a responsible member of the tribe, though in nineteenth-century New England the doctrine of free will left the individual at liberty to remain unredeemed.

In the winter of 1846, Emily's close friend Abiah Root was passing through this ordeal. She was attending a boarding school in Springfield, where she may have been under the influence of zealous teachers. She wrote to Emily about her unsettled state of mind, and received from her a prompt and sympathetic response that reveals for the first time that Emily herself was undergoing an inner struggle. Abiah's confession seems to have precipitated into an open conflict the unrest that had been smoldering for some time. Two letters from Emily to Abiah, written two months apart, provide the only source for the story of this experience. The force of the influences around her is reflected in Emily's first letter in the conventional phrases she uses. It is the voice of collective demand, rather than Emily's own, that says, "How ungrateful I am to live along day by day upon Christ's bounty and still be in a state of enmity to him." Yet the sincerity of her motive is clear when she tells her friend that she once came close to finding her Saviour, and had "never enjoyed such perfect peace and happiness." It was a real experience, too, of which she spoke when she told how she had fallen away again from this condition, and now found an aching void in her heart. Emily's own sense of reality appears, when, after telling Abiah of the revival meetings of the previous winter, she says, "Perhaps you will not believe it Dear A. but I attended none of the meetings last winter. I felt that I was so easily excited that I might again be deceived, and I dared not trust myself." Following this display of her good judgment, however, the cant phrases recur, in such expressions as "I feel that life is short and time is fleeting — and that I ought to make my peace with my maker." She concludes the first letter, "Although I am not a christian still I feel deeply the importance of attending to the subject before it is too late."

The second letter, written two months later than the first, shows even greater intensity. After hearing from Abiah that she had "found a Saviour," Emily wrote, "I feel that I am sailing upon the brink of an awful precipice, from which I cannot escape & over which I fear my tiny boat will soon glide if I do not receive help from above." Her distress is summed up in the sentence, "Surely it is a fearful thing to live & a very fearful thing to die & give up our account to the supreme ruler for all our sinful deeds & thoughts upon this probationary term of existence."

In both letters the subject of death fills a large place. She tells Abiah of the overwhelming impression that had been made on her two years before by the death of Sophia Holland, a girl of her own age to whom she felt particularly close. It was the first incursion of death among her own circle of friends, and the effect was so deep that she could not speak of it to anyone. Her parents, however, always watchful of her health, noticed her suffering and sent her to Boston to visit her Aunt Lavinia, a gentle person of whom she was very fond. Now she felt constrained to imagine the scene of her own death and to picture the state of endlessness she and her friends would experience. "Does not Eternity appear dreadful to you," she asks. "I often get thinking of it and it seems so dark to me that I almost wish there was no Eternity." We find here the feeling of the little girl pictured in the poem, "It would have starved a Gnat," longing "To gad" her "little Being out – And not begin again." It is Emily's own voice that speaks in these passages as she begins her life-long search for a relation to the unanswerable questions of life and death.

In spite of the lavish use in these letters of language caught from the pulpit, there is no doubt that Emily was suffering. Since an adolescent mind often shows uneven growth, on one side she was still, at fifteen, an obedient child, giving respect for what she had been taught. At the same time her rapidly developing intellect was reaching out for its own answers, while emotionally she was awakening to the call to participate in life's involvements. If something in her enjoyed the dramatic images with which she pictured her own dangerous condition, something else was genuinely envious of those who had found peace through submission. She seems really to have believed that she was bad, but to be herself was more compelling than to conform. The conflict was not actually centered in the issue in which she saw it at the time, but in the greater problem of the individual seeking to find himself within a collective order. For one who is to become an artist the struggle can be especially intense and painful, even though he has no means of understanding his own situation. Emily was aware of certain inner forces urging her in opposite directions, but as yet she had no basis for evaluating them other than the accepted mores of her social circle. There is no indication that Emily's parents put any pressure upon her in these circumstances. Even if Edward Dickinson had known what was happening in his young daughter's mind, which is highly improbable, he would certainly not have pushed her to any decision since he had never acknowledged his own faith publicly by becoming a member of the church he attended regularly. He was a man who would refrain from any action unless he could give himself wholly to it, and it was not until 1850, when he was forty-seven years old, that Squire Dickinson stood up with the many young and obscure persons who made their confession that summer before the congregation, and declared his repentance and the submission of his will to God.

In his austerity Emily's father may have seemed remote, but he was not unfeeling, and both her parents must have been aware that something was wrong. They had kept her at home from school during the fall term, and in the winter of 1846 her studies were limited to German and music. But when spring came she returned to school, to take the full course in preparation for entering Mount Holyoke Seminary. A letter to Abiah, written the twenty-sixth of June, tells with great enthusiasm about her plans, but does not tell how this fulfillment of a dream had come about. Whether or not her parents took the initiative in the decision, they were wise enough to see that a change was called for in which Emily's mind would be fully occupied. Her letter is in a wholly different mood from those written in the winter. The insoluble problem had been shelved, and life had taken on new meaning as all her energies became involved in the processes of intellectual growth. When her health again gave way and she had to leave school after eleven weeks of over-eager studying, her illness may have been due quite as much to the emotional strain of the preceding winter as to the work of the spring. Her search for Heaven through the conventional route had brought her only spiritual anxiety, and the road of intellectual achievement that had come as a release to the energies she had tried to subdue proved too much for her physical stamina. She wrote to Abiah in September, "I left school & did nothing for some time excepting to ride & roam in the fields." The remarkable herbarium of pressed flowers that still testifies not only to her love for the earth but to her diligent search for its treasures, was presumably collected in large part during that summer. The balance was restored, and for the ensuing year there was no hint of doom in her letters.

During the year at Mount Holyoke Seminary, which she entered in the autumn of 1847, the pressure was renewed, since the state of every girl's soul was scrutinized with as much care as was given to the examination of her acquired knowledge. The conflict returned in full force. Emily sincerely tried to feel what others felt, but was too honest with herself to deny that the strongest pull came from the side she could only call "the world." Even though it cost her dearly, she had the courage to stand alone in a situation that brought her a wretched sense of inferiority. Although the intellectual stimulus she found at Mount Holyoke still seemed to her a great privilege, as a means of reaching Heaven it proved to be a failure. The winter term was broken by illness, and she was relieved when her father decided not to send her back for another year. In the spring she wrote to Abiah Root,

I tremble when I think how soon the weeks and days of this term will all have been spent, and my fate will be sealed, perhaps. I have neglected the *one thing needful* when all were obtaining it, and I may never again pass through such a season as was granted us last winter. Abiah, you may be surprised to hear me speak as I do, knowing that I express no interest in the all-important subject, but I am not happy, and I regret that last term, when that golden opportunity was mine, that I did not give up and become a Christian. It is not now too late, so my friends tell me, so my offended conscience whispers, but it is hard for me to give up the world. I had quite a long talk with Abby while at home and I doubt not she will soon cast her burden on Christ. She is sober, and keenly sensitive on the subject, and she says she only desires to be good. How I wish I could say that with sincerity, but I fear I never can. But I will no longer impose my own feelings even upon my friend. Keep them sacred, for I never lisped them to any save yourself and Abby.

Only two letters survive from the year 1849 when Emily was at home again. Both, written to young men, were about books. These facts suggest that to be free from school routine, to read books of her own choice and discuss them with friends, to take part in the life of a group of young people from college and town, brought welcome expansion after the stricture of the disciplined life at Mount Holyoke. Above all, this was a year of importance because it marked the development of her friendship with her father's law student, Benjamin Franklin Newton.

TO LIVE IS ENDOWMENT

If the few passages in Emily's letters referring to Newton are put together, they form an account of their friendship as intense as it is brief, for each one carries such weight that the relation with him is seen as one of the most significant in her entire life. At a time when a new impetus was needed to enable her to free herself from the demands of orthodoxy and to bring into its own the spirit that in self-defense had been forced to play the part of Satan, Newton, who was ten years her senior, brought new values that showed her the way to becoming a poet. Their association at Amherst lasted scarcely more than a year, for Newton returned to his home in Worcester before the end of 1849. During the remainder of his short life, however, they corresponded, and we may surmise that she sent him the verses she wrote. The only records of what he meant to her are a few allusions to him in some of her letters.

In the beginning of her correspondence with Thomas Wentworth Higginson, twelve years after Newton left Amherst, Mr. Higginson attempted to discover how she had come to write her startling poems. In answering his questions she gave first place in the development of her mind to Newton's influence. "When I was a little Girl," she said, as she always did in later years in speaking of herself up to the middle twenties, "I had a friend who taught me Immortality – but venturing too near, himself, he never returned – Soon after, my Tutor died – and for several years, my Lexicon – was my only companion." Later, when Higginson praised the poems she had sent, her reply adds certainty to the implication that Newton had encouraged her writing. "My dying

Tutor told me that he would like to live till I had been a poet,
but Death was much of Mob as I could master – then – And
when far afterward – a sudden light on Orchards, or a new
fashion in the wind troubled my attention – I felt a palsy,
here – the Verses just relieve." The ecstatic moments Emily
thus described to Higginson had probably come to her always,
stirring into consciousness the sense of loss she recurrently
felt. In Newton she must have found for the first time a person with whom she dared to share something of these experiences, or who recognized in her the spark that made her different from those around her. He was a man of little formal
education, who thought and read for himself, and was able
to fan the spark into vigorous life.

During the winter of 1850, when all of Amherst was
affected by the great "awakening" that ran through the
churches, Emily's letters were ebullient with revolt. She still
looked wistfully at her friends who had found peace in their
submission to the demands of religion, but her fear that she
"never can" had grown into an acceptance of the side of herself she felt was opposed to it. She still sought Abiah's prayers,
but to Jane Humphrey she confessed, "I am standing alone
in rebellion, and growing very careless. Abby, Mary, Jane,
and farthest of all my Vinnie have been seeking, and they
all believe they have found; I cant tell you *what* they have
found, but *they* think it is something precious. I wonder if it
is?" Her rebellion extended to the omission of good works, as
exemplified by the young women of Amherst. She told Jane
Humphrey:

The Sewing Society has commenced again – and held its first meeting last week – now all the poor will be helped – the cold warmed – the warm cooled – the hungry fed – the thirsty attended to – the ragged clothed – and this suffering – tumbled down world will be helped to it's feet again – which will be quite pleasant to all. I dont attend – notwithstanding my high approbation – which must puzzle the public exceedingly. I am already set down as one of those brands almost consumed – and my hardheartedness gets me many prayers.

Vitality pulsates through the letters, finding expression in gay nonsense that occasionally shades off into irony. To the pious Abiah she found it necessary to explain that the long flight of fancy she had just read on being possessed by a cold was "vain imaginations to lead astray foolish young women. They are flowers of speech, they both *make,* and *tell* deliberate falsehoods, avoid them as the snake, and turn aside as from the *Bottle* snake, and I dont *think* you will be harmed." Some of her avowals of wickedness were transparent declarations of defiance of the orthodox view of life. To Jane Humphrey she wrote, "The path of duty looks very ugly indeed – and the place where *I* want to go more amiable – a great deal – it is so much easier to do wrong than right – so much pleasanter to be evil than good, I dont wonder that good angels weep – and bad ones sing songs."

A year of social gaiety seems to have run concomitantly with the religious fervor in the community, and Emily made new friends. Newton had left Amherst, but his place in her life was special and secure. In the spring she wrote Abiah about "a friend I love *so* dearly," whose invitation to a drive she had sadly and bitterly refused because of her duty to her ailing mother, ridiculing herself meanwhile for her excessive suffering over a small disappointment that ended when she "came to" her "various senses in great dudgeon at life, and time, and love for affliction, and anguish."

Behind all these contrasting moods lay an intense emotional experience, of which there are only a few hints contained in two letters during the spring of 1850. To Jane Humphrey, in whom she would have liked to confide had they been together, she said,

I would whisper to you in the evening of many, and curious things — and by the lamps eternal read your thoughts and response in your face, and find what you thought about me, and what I have done, and am doing; I know you would be surprised, whether in pleasure, or disappointment it does'nt become me to say – I have dared to do strange things — bold things, and have asked no advice from any — I have heeded beautiful tempters, yet do not think I am wrong. Oh I have needed my trusty Jane — my friend encourager, and sincere counciller, my rock, and strong assister! I could make you tremble for me, and be very much afraid, and wonder how things would end – Oh Jennie, it would relieve me to tell you all, to sit down at your feet, and look in your eyes, and confess what *you only* shall know, an experience bitter, and sweet, but the sweet did so beguile me — and life has had an aim, and the world has been too precious for your poor — and striving sister! The winter was all one dream, and the spring has not yet waked me, I would *always* sleep, and dream, and it never should turn to morning, so long as night is so blessed. What do you weave from all these threads, for I know you hav'nt been idle the while I've been speaking to you, bring it nearer the window, and I will see, it's all wrong unless it has one gold thread in it, a long, big shining fibre which hides the others — and which will fade away into Heaven while you hold it, and from there come back to me. I hope belief is not wicked, and assurance, and perfect trust — and a kind of twilight feeling before the moon is seen – I hope human nature has truth in it – Oh I pray it may not deceive – confide – cherish, have a great faith in — do you dream from all this what I mean? Nobody *thinks* of the joy, nobody *guesses* it, to all appearance old things are engrossing, and new ones are not revealed, but there *now* is nothing old, things are budding, and springing, and singing, and you rather think you are in a green grove, and it's branches that go, and come.

To Abiah, in explanation of her failure to write, she explained,

> Where do you think I've strayed, and from what new errand returned? I have come from *"to* and *fro,* and walking up, and down" the same place that Satan hailed from, when God asked him where he'd been, but not to illustrate further I tell you I have been dreaming, dreaming a *golden* dream, with eyes all the while wide open, and I guess it's almost morning, and besides I have been at work, providing the "food that perisheth," scaring the timorous dust, and being obedient, and kind.

This letter to Jane Humphrey has come to light since George F. Whicher wrote in *This Was a Poet* about the various highly colored versions of a legend current in Amherst during Emily's life concerning an early attachment to a young man that was broken up by her father after the discovery of clandestine meetings. Certainly these passages suggest a basis for such an episode. Emily was nineteen; her sensibilities were acutely active and her emotions easily stirred. She was not finding treasure in Heaven in the prescribed manner, and might have glimpsed it potentially in a relation with a young man. If she did, the experience had no direct connection with her later retirement from the life of the community, as the legends assumed. Indeed, her own involvement could hardly have been more than tentative, since she speaks of it as a dream, and implies in the letter to Abiah that she knows the dream may evaporate when morning comes.

No more is heard of the dream, but since it disappeared without leaving any discernible damage, it presumably fulfilled a function in Emily's development. Holding this point of view one can construct a wholly different interpretation of these passages. In one sense, Emily did remain, as she said of herself, a "little girl" until she was well into the years of maturity, for it was not until her thirtieth year that her awakening as a woman brought her into the full stream of her life as a poet. When she wrote to Abiah that spring of "a friend I love *so* dearly," she would not have expected her to infer that the young man was her lover. The word "love" was given wide application at that time, and sentiment was freely expressed, even between men. Congeniality of mind drew Emily most strongly. Under the guidance of Ben Newton, she had probably begun already to attempt some writing of her own. In January 1850, soon after he had left Amherst, she told Jane Humphrey that she had received a letter and a copy of Emerson's poems from him, commenting, "I should love to read you them both – they are very pleasant to me. I can write him in about three weeks – and I *shall*." Why her writing to him was limited to certain intervals she did not explain, but the inference is that her correspondence with him was not encouraged by her parents. Could the "strange things – bold things" she had dared to do have been no more audacious than breaking the parental command to write secretly to the man whose mind had so stimulated her, and whom she could trust when she sent him her verses and arranged to receive his criticisms? "I have heeded beautiful tempters, yet do not think I am wrong," she said, and "life has had an aim." The joy she felt — "things are budding, and springing, and singing" — could be the effect of a burst of creative energy under the encouragement of an admired and trusted friend. Whether the winter's dream was personal and erotic, or whether it sprang from the inner world of a creative mind, it marked a turning point in Emily's road toward the goal of finding her "delinquent palaces." She knew now that, whatever her failure might be in the eyes of others, or even in the sight of the God she had been taught to acknowledge, she could not do else than be herself in all honesty, and seek her own values with sincere devotion.

Outside of Emily's own comments on her friendship with Ben Newton, nothing is known of his personality or of his feeling for the girl he had been privileged to lead so perceptively. A year and a half after he left Amherst, when he was already in poor health, he married an older woman who nursed him until his death two years later. Yet Emily, in whose response to his leadership he must have found an answer to a need of his own, seems to have held an important place in his life to the end. Years later, in a letter to Higginson she wrote, "My earliest friend wrote me the week before he died 'If I live, I will go to Amherst – if I die, I certainly will.'" When she heard of his death, in March 1853, her only allusion to him in her letters appears in a postscript to Austin like a sharp cry — "Oh Austin, Newton is dead. The first of my own friends. Pace." Her sense of loss must have been augmented by her inability to talk freely of him with anyone, for, nearly a year later, she wrote to a complete stranger, the Reverend Edward Everett Hale of Worcester, asking whether he had been her friend's pastor. She explained that Mr. Newton had become for her "a gentle, yet grave Preceptor," teaching her "what to read, what authors to admire, what was most grand or beautiful in nature, and that sublimer lesson, a faith in things unseen, and in a life again, nobler, and much more blessed." She longed to know whether he had been "willing to die," and whether his pastor thought him "at Home" in Heaven. Her concern over the manner of her friend's death and his future life must have been less a matter of anxiety for his soul than of reassurance in regard to his teaching on immortality. It was he who had helped to free her from the bonds imposed on her by the orthodox views of Heaven and Hell, introducing her to Emerson and other writers who had broadened her horizon.

In the close-knit society of a small and still Puritanical college town, freedom could come to her only through inward isolation. Young women did not leave home except for marriage, or to earn their living by teaching. Edward Dickinson provided well for his family, protected them from the rough world, and expected compliance in his plans. Emily complied, and her daily life during the years of her early maturity was regulated by family loyalty, parental authority, and the demands of household routine.

During the years when her brother Austin was away from home, first teaching in Boston, then studying law at Harvard, Emily wrote to him voluminously. She fed his homesickness with so many vivid and amusing pictures of life at Amherst and such constant laments over his absence that the reader might draw the conclusion that she was entirely involved in the life of home and town. The style she used in writing to him, however, may not have been indicative of her general state of mind. Gay mockery and a humorous view of life are sometimes weapons with which a person who is pained or disturbed defends himself from despondency. It is true that her home was very dear to Emily, and that her tie to the brother and sister who always accepted her fully was very strong, but there was also a negative element involved in her clinging so closely. The outside world was becoming harder and harder to deal with. She no longer attended the Sewing Circle. She still went to church with the family, and "witnessed a couple of Baptisms, three admissions to church, a Supper of the Lord, and some other minor transactions," but her spirit, armed with detachment, remained outside. She did take part in the meetings of a young people's reading club and had tea with her friends, but large public gatherings she already looked upon with horror.

The letters to Austin never quite reached the pitch of satire, for she was writing with warm affection to a young man who wanted to hear what was going on at home, but who dearly loved a joke. In December 1851, she wrote:

When I know of anything funny, I am just as apt to cry, far *more* so than to *laugh*, for I know who *loves jokes best*, and who is not here to enjoy them. We dont *have* many jokes tho' *now*, it is pretty much all sobriety, and we do not have much poetry, father having made up his mind that its pretty much all *real life*. Fathers real life and *mine* sometimes come into collision, but as yet, escape unhurt!

Emily's own real life, as opposed to her father's, may have remained unrecognized by him, even though she felt his opposition keenly. Affection for friends would have been understood, but a desire for intangibles such as Emily sought had no part in the daily round. Since she often sat up late to write to Austin, she may also have sat up late to write the verses that led Newton to hope he might live to see her a poet. But the search was not confined to an attempt at self-expression. In her longing for spiritual companionship she sometimes saw in a particular person an effulgence that was really of her own making. The little notes of love she sent to Emily Fowler, an admired friend a few years older than she, are clearly the expression of a feeling of this sort. When Austin became interested in Susan Gilbert, Emily's heart followed his, and the separation from Sue when she was teaching in Baltimore tended to make her endow her friend with values too great to be borne. "Oh Susie," she wrote in February 1852, "I would nestle close to your warm heart, and never hear the wind blow, or the storm beat, again." Later in the same letter the personification in Sue of a spiritual value is clearly expressed when she tells of how she waked in the night saying, "Precious treasure, thou art mine." It is probable that on Sue's return, when the girls were often together, their intimacy developed on terms that were controlled by Sue's more factual mind.

By the time Emily met Dr. and Mrs. Holland, a year or so later, she was able to shed on them some of the glory with which she had invested Sue, and even to see, with her protective sense of humor, how the exuberance of her delight in her new friends might appear to them. In an effusive letter written in the autumn of 1853, she said, "If it wasn't for broad daylight, and cooking-stoves, and roosters, I'm afraid you would have occasion to smile at my letters often, but so sure as 'this mortal' essays immortality, a crow from a neighboring farm-yard dissipates the illusion, and I am here again." The Hollands may have been puzzled by Emily's use of the word "immortality," which they would have associated only with life after death, but they could not have missed the implication that her elation must be brought down to earth. Searching always in nature, in friendship, or within her own being, for the source of the unknown treasure she occasionally glimpsed but never clearly saw, she had found in the word "immortality" an expression of the enlargement of spirit these ecstatic moments brought. She conceived of it, not as projected into a future life, but as something present, though separated from the reality of every day, and carrying with it an awareness of a larger self. Her use of the word was less Christian than Greek, for the godlike feeling that came to her made her one with the immortals.

During her middle twenties, Emily's life was outwardly the normal one of a young woman living at home. She baked and sewed, made rounds of social calls with her sister, and maintained several friendships. She had her private joys in her garden, her walks with her dog, her books, and her writing. Yet the letters of these years, taken as a whole, leave the impression that she lived tentatively, and with an increasing division between the inner and the outer worlds. There was still a sense of lack that kept her in a precarious state of balance. She was in constant dread of losing her friends. Newton was already gone, and a friendship with an Amherst student, Henry Vaughn Emmons, based on mutual tastes, was of short duration. Even the temporary absence of those she loved produced a fear of desertion. Her clinging love must have become irksome to Sue, for Emily, in a letter in 1854, showed that she was so hurt by something Sue had said that she believed their friendship had come to an end. Emily defended herself by taking refuge in angry defiance expressed in terms of dramatic resignation. It is hard to untangle the personal hurt from the injury to the spirit she felt she had received from Sue's sharp criticism. She was touched to the quick when she wrote,

> Sue — I have lived by this. It is the lingering emblem of the Heaven I once dreamed, and though if this is taken, I shall remain alone, and though in that last day, the Jesus Christ you love, remark he does not know me — there is a darker spirit will not disown it's child.

Since Emily had said earlier in the letter, "We differ often lately," one might infer that the disagreement lay in the girls' religious views, but the next paragraph seems to indicate that it was the intensity of the friendship itself that Sue had found unbearable.

> Few have been given me, and if I love them so, that for *idolatry* they are removed from me — I simply murmur *gone*, and the billow dies away into the boundless blue, and no one knows but me, that one went down today. We have walked very pleasantly — Perhaps this is the point at which our paths diverge — then pass on singing Sue, and up the distant hill I journey on.

The girls' intimate friendship appears to have had no interruption, though Sue, who was now engaged to Austin and had a superior commitment, continued to disappoint Emily by her lack of response. The poem with which this letter closed left the way open for a renewal of the friendship on a new basis, as well as for a new phase in the writer's own growth. "I have a Bird in spring" may not have been written for the occasion, but its message was appropriate, for the first two stanzas carry out the image of the flown bird that

> Learneth beyond the sea
> Melody new for me
> And will return.

The episode involved far more than the actual relation between the two young women. Sue had touched with her criticism something deeply meaningful to Emily, but of which she was probably not yet fully aware, as she struggled to find her identity. It is not possible to follow this inner struggle, for the content of it is not revealed, either in this letter, which shows only a surface manifestation, or the few that succeed it in the years immediately following.

Something is known of the outer events, if not of the inner developments of her life at this time, for there were several important occurrences. In 1855 Emily made her last effort to take part in the social world, when she and Lavinia went with their father to Washington, and visited old friends in Philadelphia. There, presumably, she met the Reverend Charles Wadsworth, who became one of the most important figures in her life — though whether as the lover she must renounce as well as the beloved counselor on whose understanding she relied during most of her remaining years is a question that may never be satisfactorily answered. The same year brought an upheaval when the Dickinson family moved from the house in which Emily had grown up back to the family mansion. Austin and Sue were married the following summer and built the house next door. And, through much of that time Mrs. Dickinson was in such poor health that Emily was more closely confined to daily tasks than she had ever been.

Although she walked firmly in the path of duty, Emily's emotions fluctuated. Changes of mood are reflected in the few surviving letters of 1855 and 1856. In some instances she seems to have proclaimed an inner holiday as she turned to her friends for release of spirit. She shared her lighter moments wth them, as when she gave Mrs. Holland a description of the effect of moving. "I took at the time a memorandum of my several senses, and also of my hat and coat, and my best shoes — but it was lost in the *mêlée*, and I am out with lanterns, looking for myself. Such wits as I reserved, are so badly shattered that repair is useless — and still I can't help laughing at my own catastrophe." In another mood, such freshets of love seemed to be welling up in her that she could find no outlet large enough for them except in a paradise containing all her friends. Yet, woven among the expressions of joy in nature, love of her friends, and thoughts of Heaven, is a fine web of disenchantment, of things fading and broken, of loss, and change, and disappearance.

After telling of her mother's puzzling condition, Emily describes herself to Mrs. Holland as "but a simple child, and frightened at myself." She continues, "I often wish I was a grass, or a toddling daisy, whom all these problems of the dust might not terrify." To steady herself in a confusing world, she had probably begun a correspondence with Dr. Wadsworth, for by the time he came to see her, several years later, a relation was firmly established between them. The one letter from him that remained with her papers, though undated, appears to be concerned with the crisis in her life that began about 1860. Although he misspelled her name, he signed himself, "Sincerely and most Affectionately, *Yours-*", as an old and tried friend.

It is perhaps fitting that at the close of Emily Dickinson's prolonged girlhood there should be a year of which she has left no record. No manuscripts, either verse or prose, can with assurance be dated 1857. It is possible that during that year she had a serious illness, for certain poems that she copied in 1858 and 1859 appear to have been written from the point of view of a person who thought she would soon die. There is nothing to prove such a conjecture, and if it is assumed that the poems were composed at the time the handwriting indicates, they can be interpreted quite differently. However obscure the outlines of that year may be, it must be regarded as a time of transition at the close of a phase of her life, and a preparation for the new and crucial period that was soon to begin. Already her small figure was somewhat separated from the community by her inability to conform to its accepted standards. The delight with which she reached out to the few friends with whom she felt secure gave welcome relief, but could not remove the burden she carried of unlived emotions. The terror she felt even of the exigencies of life at home was a part of the division between the inner and outer worlds. The patterns that were developing below the level of consciousness were disturbing enough to give her a sense of instability without making themselves directly felt. It is not surprising that in the years immediately following she wrote several poems about volcanoes, and used the same image in a number of poems on other subjects. Out of this dark period she emerged with more definiteness in the year 1858, when the assembling of the first packets of poems marked the beginning of the real flowering of her creative genius.

OURSELF BEHIND OURSELF

An interpretation of the crisis
in the life of Emily Dickinson

Among the poems that Emily Dickinson gathered together in 1858, many are immature and sentimental and may have had an earlier origin. Some show her close and loving observation of nature, but there are few that approach in quality the power of feeling and expression that was released in the years immediately following.

A few, however, seem to have sprung from the moods that are felt when the inner stirring of something unknown brings a strong sense of impending calamity. There are suggestions in some of the poems that she feared she was going to die. The sudden realization that life may cease at any moment is probably a common experience of late adolescence, and in her protected life Emily at twenty-seven had scarcely passed some of the phases of that period. During her long girlhood, spent in a house where the windows looked down on the grave-yard, she had lived in daily awareness of death, and, in mourning the loss of two young men who had been important to her, had come to feel the insecurity of the tenure of life. But there is something more specific than this in the verses

"I often passed the village" and "I hav'nt told my garden yet." In the first she dwells on the atmosphere of the grave-yard, and says:

> I did not know the year then –
> In which my call would come –
> Earlier, by the Dial,
> Than the rest have gone.

Since there is no record of a serious illness at this time, her premonition seems to be of the same nature as the dreams of dying that often presage a change in the life of the mind, when inner growth demands that a familiar part of the self give place to the new.

In another group of the poems of 1858, Emily used the sea as a symbol. Universally understood to represent the unknown — whether in the human adventure it stands for life, death, or eternity — the sea may also mean the unknown depths and distances within the human soul. So far as is known, Emily never saw the sea, and she never wrote of it descriptively, as she did of the hills around Amherst. To her it was always a symbol, and at this time it was chiefly associated with the danger of shipwreck. She was still afloat on its surface, not engulfed in it, but her little vessel was in imminent danger.

> Adrift! A little boat adrift!
> And night is coming down!
> Will *no* one guide a little boat
> Unto the nearest town?
>
> So Sailors say – on yesterday –
> Just as the dusk was brown
> One little boat gave up it's strife
> And gurgled down and down.

TO LIVE IS ENDOWMENT

So angels say – on yesterday –
Just as the dawn was red
One little boat – o'erspent with gales –
Retrimmed it's masts – redecked it's sails –
And shot – exultant on!

The sailors and the angels, who see the calamity from opposite points of view, may represent the division she was beginning to feel within herself. In another poem, putting herself in the place of Noah, she sends out her spirit as the puzzled dove seeking for land.

Once more, my now bewildered Dove
Bestirs her puzzled wings
Once more her mistress, on the deep
Her troubled question flings –

Thrice to the floating casement
The Patriarch's bird returned,
Courage! My brave Columba!
There may yet be *Land*!

With her whole world in the grip of a great flood that she does not understand, she is consciously seeking an answer with courage and determination.

In the poems of 1859 the stress of soul becomes more intense, taking form in different moods and attempts to interpret them. The danger and uncertainty of the little boat on the sea are still present in " 'Twas such a little – little boat," but in another poem using the sea image a new note is struck.

Exultation is the going
Of an inland soul to sea,
Past the houses – past the headlands –
Into deep Eternity –

OURSELF BEHIND OURSELF

> Bred as we, among the mountains,
> Can the sailor understand
> The divine intoxication
> Of the first league out from land?

Instead of fearing shipwreck, she is now positively impelled toward the sea, which she identifies with eternity. That "Eternity" here means the life after death seems doubtful, because at the same time she was writing poems about heaven that follow the earlier conception of a paradise built on traditional lines. More probable is a meaning similar to that given earlier to "immortality," signifying wholeness of life contained in the great mystery of the inner world.

Among the other moods that appear in poems of the time is rebelliousness. Emily ridicules the behavior induced by the demands of society, which force the individual to assume a mask.

> To hang our head – ostensibly –
> And subsequent, to find
> That such was not the posture
> Of our immortal mind –
>
> Affords the sly presumption
> That in so dense a fuzz –
> You – too – take Cobweb attitudes
> Upon a plane of Gauze!

In "A little East of Jordan" she tells the story of Jacob wrestling with the angel, which concludes with these lines:

> And the bewildered Gymnast
> Found he had worsted God!

Emily also is fighting an unknown antagonist who might be

revealed as the representative of the God of her Fathers, and she is frightened lest, like Jacob, she might find she had prevailed over him.

A third poem shows her to be almost ready to venture all, even her own soul, to gain the unknown goal that she longs for but fears.

> Soul, Wilt thou toss again?
> By just such a hazard
> Hundreds have lost indeed –
> But tens have won an all –
>
> Angels' breathless ballot
> Lingers to record thee –
> Imps in eager Caucus
> Raffle for my Soul!

The theme of imprisonment and escape appears in two poems of the same year. That beginning

> I never hear the word "escape"
> Without a quicker blood,

ends in defeat

> But I tug childish at my bars
> Only to fail again!

A poem in another mood is about the happy escape of a butterfly from its chrysalis ("Cocoon above! Cocoon below!"), an image that was to appear several times in succeeding years.

In 1859 she also became aware of a figure met in dreams, who had the power to control her happiness. The poem beginning "I have a King, who does not speak" might be an expression of a girl's feeling for a man with whom she has fallen in love, but who as yet remains remote from her. The emotional tone of the poem, however, seems more in keeping with a different interpretation. The mysterious silence of the dream king and the happiness brought by a vision of him suggest that the figure is purely symbolic. Under his domination daily life becomes meaningful, but she can maintain contact with him only in the unconsciousness of sleep.

> I have a King, who does not speak –
> So – wondering – thro' the hours meek
> I trudge the day away –
> Half glad when it is night, and sleep,
> If, haply, thro' a dream, to peep
> In parlors, shut by day.
>
> And if I do – when morning comes –
> It is as if a hundred drums
> Did round my pillow roll,
> And shouts fill all my Childish sky,
> And Bells keep saying "Victory"
> From steeples in my soul!
>
> And if I dont — the little Bird
> Within the Orchard, is not heard,
> And I omit to pray
> "Father, thy will be done" today
> For my will goes the other way,
> And it were perjury!

The dreamer's allegiance now goes to an inner authority, whose claims are recognized as of greater force than those of the human father or the father God of whom he is the representative. In the new symbol, not yet identified as a lover but as a monarch, Emily instinctively acknowledges the power within herself of the masculine principle, which in complementing her own femineity is to play a leading role in her development as woman and poet. Although she is still unaware of what is happening, the stage is set for the next act, in which she is to take part both as actor and observer.

By 1860 the real work of the poet had begun. A liberation of the creative force found expression in a wide range of subjects and variations of mood, but the year is notable as the first in which appear poems on the theme of love.

In a mood of retrospection the poet takes stock of the values stored up in her past, only to find they have vanished.

> I cautious, scanned my little life –
> I winnowed what would fade
> From what w'd last till Heads like mine
> Should be a-dreaming laid.
>
> I put the latter in a Barn –
> The former, blew away.
> I went one winter morning
> And lo – my priceless Hay
>
> Was not upon the "Scaffold" –
> Was not upon the "Beam" –
> And from a thriving Farmer –
> A Cynic, I became.
>
> Whether a Thief did it –
> Whether it was the wind –
> Whether Deity's guiltless –
> My business is, to find!
>
> So I begin to ransack!
> How is it Hearts, with Thee?
> Art thou within the little Barn
> Love provided Thee?

She suspects that this loss may be the work of God, and is even doubtful whether her own heart is contained within the frame she had built for it. The emptiness leaves room, however, for new and greater values to come in.

Maturity cannot come all at once, and childish moods alternate with struggle in the search for herself. At about this time she wrote the poem "We dont cry – Tim and I" in which she returned to the unseen playmate of her childhood. This seeming retrogression to the attitude of a little girl is in striking contrast to another poem containing two figures. The setting is again the sea, but this time no little boat floats on its surface, for the shipwreck has already occurred, and nothing is left but a single spar for the victims to cling to.

> Two swimmers wrestled on the spar –
> Until the morning sun –
> When One – turned smiling to the land –
> Oh God! the Other One!
>
> The stray ships – passing –
> Spied a face –
> Upon the waters borne –
> With eyes in death – still begging raised –
> And hands – beseeching – thrown!

It is as if two parts of a divided self were fighting for survival.

One cannot help associating with this last poem a second, which has been found only in the handwriting of 1862, about two years later than that of the two swimmers, but which bears every indication of belonging to the same period, or of having been written in recollection of it.

> Three times – we parted – Breath – and I –
> Three times – He would not go –

But strove to stir the lifeless Fan
The Waters – strove to stay.

Three Times – the Billows threw me up –
Then caught me – like a Ball –
Then made Blue faces in my face –
And pushed away a sail

That crawled Leagues off – I liked to see –
For thinking – while I die –
How pleasant to behold a Thing
Where Human faces – be –

The Waves grew sleepy – Breath – did not –
The Winds – like Children – lulled –
Then Sunrise kissed my Chrysalis –
And I stood up – and lived –

Instead of an unidentified swimmer her conscious self is now buffeted and in acute danger of drowning. But "Breath" — which is life itself — will not let her go. The danger passes without any effort on her part, and a curious change in imagery comes as the sea loses its terrifying aspect. She is now a butterfly emerging from a chrysalis at the touch of the sun. A new phase of life has begun. In the two poems "At last, to be identified!" and "Tho' I get home how late – how late," she felt that her identity was established, and she could look forward with hope, though life's journey might be long and fulfillment reached only in Heaven. The movement is forward, and an arrival is predicted, in spite of the difficulties to be met.

The kiss of the sunrise, that brought the butterfly out of its chrysalis, is clearly something that has happened in the external world. Into the emptiness that had placed her in such danger has come the revivifying experience of falling in love. The God she had been taught to revere had proved insufficient, and looking within she had become aware of dark and mysterious forces that might overwhelm her in her defenseless state. Into the vacuum left by her struggle had come a man who carried the attributes of a God she could adore, and who as a man had the power to bring to life the smoldering fires of the woman's instincts.

It is not necessary to identify the man who stirred Emily so profoundly. It is hardly necessary to postulate the existence of any actual man as the object of her love, so closely was her emotion connected with her own inner involvement. Yet, drafts of letters exist in handwriting of this period to someone whom she called "Master," so expressed that if the situation they imply had been wholly imaginary, they would either have been the product of an insane mind or else of one unentangled enough to fabricate consciously. Neither of these states is consistent with the impression given by other letters and the many and varied poems of the time.

The earliest of the three drafts, written about 1858, may have been intended for a different person from the one to whom she wrote the later two, in 1861 or 1862. Since she was to use the title "Master" ten years later, in writing to Thomas Wentworth Higginson, it is probable that she felt it applicable to any man to whom she looked with deep respect as an authority. Not only are the later drafts more intense in tone, but the emotion that is poured out in them is of a more erotic cast. Without doubt, the depth and intensity of her feeling were far greater than the actual facts in her relation to the man would have called forth if she had been a woman of simpler responses. The importance of the experience lay in its effect upon her, which was almost measureless.

At its central point was the encounter of Emily's conscious self with a personification of the symbol first seen in the "King, who does not speak." She was in desperate need of a savior, a mediator between her struggling consciousness and the unplumbed depths of her own nature, to bring her being into focus and enable her to experience wholeness of life. The powerful image that stepped out of dreams and manifested itself for her in a living man held godlike potentialities for setting in motion, with the aid of her own awareness, the forces of integration.

But full awareness can be reached only after full acceptance of experience as it comes through the senses and emotions. Emily Dickinson began to explore the experience of love. She still hesitated before the door:

> Come slowly – Eden!
> Lips unused to Thee –
> Bashful – sip thy Jessamines –
> As the fainting Bee –
>
> Reaching late his flower,
> Round her chamber hums –
> Counts his nectars –
> Enters – and is lost in Balms.

She played more than once with the image of the flower and the bee, giving it sexual significance in the poems, "The Flower must not blame the Bee" and "Did the Harebell loose her girdle," as she became aware of her own awakened instincts. Oblivious of convention, she gave her fantasy free rein when she wrote "He was weak, and I was strong – then." Fully alive now, and feeling herself freed from the choking restrictions that had bound her, she identified herself with a wild creature of the jungle as she ejaculated:

> With thee, in the Desert –
> With thee in the thirst –
> With thee in the Tamarind wood –
> Leopard breathes – at last!

The theme of venturing all upon a throw, which she had left an open question a year earlier in the poem "Soul, Wilt thou toss again," reappeared at this time in a mood of exultant daring when she wrote three stanzas sprinkled with exclamation points, beginning:

> 'Tis so much joy! 'Tis so much joy!
> If I should fail, what poverty!

She weighs the consequences of taking the supreme risk, and accepts even failure itself as of value, because "to know the worst, is sweet!" For the time the stimulating effect of a vivid emotion was enough — life was expanding and brimming with hope, and the creative fire was burning strongly. It was at this time she wrote:

> I taste a liquor never brewed –
> From Tankards scooped in Pearl –
> Not all the Frankfort Berries
> Yield such an Alcohol!
>
> Inebriate of Air – am I –
> And Debauchee of Dew –
> Reeling – thro endless summer days –
> From inns of Molten Blue –

TO LIVE IS ENDOWMENT

When "Landlords" turn the drunken Bee
Out of the Foxglove's door –
When Butterflies – renounce their "drams" –
I shall but drink the more!

Till Seraphs swing their snowy Hats –
And Saints – to windows run –
To see the little Tippler
From Manzanilla come!

"Reeling – thro endless summer days" describes a condition
that life does not long permit, and a conflict between such an
ecstatic state of inflation and the world of fact could hardly
be avoided. Something shattered the spell under which Emily
was held. There came a point beyond which she could not go
without carrying the emotion into a real relation with the
person who had called it forth. Since many things point to
an assumption that the loved one was a married man, the
shock probably came when, by some word of his or a sudden
revelation of her own intuition, she was forced to accept the
reality of the situation. The miraculous condition of being in
love fosters belief in infinite possibilities that bear no relation
to fact, and in which the moral sense remains totally blind.
If Emily suddenly became aware of what she had been wishing, her conscious attitude would have reinforced the inevi-
tability of her fate. Ten years later she was to write, with
knowledge of her own tendency to escape from reality:

I bet with every Wind that blew
Till Nature in chagrin
Employed a Fact to visit me
And scuttle my Balloon –

It is not surprising that in 1861 Emily Dickinson's handwriting showed great agitation. She wrote voluminously, on many subjects and in many moods, living, perhaps, on several levels or in different compartments of her psychic house, while the foundations began to shake underneath. In a mood of delight in life itself she could write of revelry in "We – Bee and I – live by the quaffing," then in deepest gloom cry out:

If *He dissolve* – then – there is *nothing – more –*
Eclipse – at *Midnight –*
It was *dark – before –*

Sunset – at *Easter –*
Blindness – on the *Dawn –*
Faint Star of Bethlehem –
Gone down!

Would but some *God – inform* Him –
Or it be *too late!*
Say – that the pulse *just lisps –*
The *Chariots wait –*

Say – that a *little life –* for *His –*
Is *leaking – red –*
His little *Spaniel –* tell Him!
Will He heed?

Such extremes are danger signals pointing to a serious un-balance. The abject dependence of the spaniel on its master, whose very existence is so uncertain that he may dissolve entirely away, is far removed from the partnership in love described in the lines "Forever at His side to walk," written in the same year, and the active devotion expressed in another contemporary poem, "Doubt Me! My Dim Companion!" The "Dim Companion" has become completely unreal, and threatens to dissolve altogether, taking with him the whole of Emily's life force. She even thinks of suicide as a means of rejoining the lover who has ceased to exist for her in the real world.

> What if I say I shall not wait!
> What if I burst the fleshly Gate –
> And pass escaped – to thee!

At the climax of this desperate condition, it seemed as if something in her had actually died.

> I felt a Funeral, in my Brain,
> And Mourners to and fro
> Kept treading – treading – till it seemed
> That Sense was breaking through –
>
> And when they all were seated,
> A Service, like a Drum –
> Kept beating – beating – till I thought
> My Mind was going numb –
>
> And then I heard them lift a Box
> And creak across my Soul
> With those same Boots of Lead, again,
> Then Space – began to toll,
>
> As all the Heavens were a Bell,
> And Being, but an Ear,
> And I, and Silence, some strange Race
> Wrecked, solitary, here –
>
> And then a Plank in Reason, broke,
> And I dropped down, and down –
> And hit a World, at every plunge,
> And Finished knowing – then –

With the horror of finding that her last hold on reality had given way, she was plunged into the merciful void of un-consciousness, where contact with the roots of being might once more be found. The extraordinary clarity with which she was able to record the experience shows that she did not pass beyond the border of sanity, for the insane cannot explain themselves; but there must have been a period when it was only with the greatest difficulty that she could withstand the disintegrating forces that assailed her. There is a vast difference, however, between the helplessness described in the last poem and the attitude of conscious acceptance in one beginning "Alone, I cannot be," for in the end the figures of fantasy and dream were the means of her salvation. With intense condensation and clarity she described the coming above the threshold of consciousness of a visiting host, un-identifiable, uncontrollable, but not malign. There is wonder, but no terror in this poem.

> Alone, I cannot be –
> The Hosts – do visit me –
> Recordless Company –
> Who baffle Key –
>
> They have no Robes, nor Names –
> No Almanacs – nor Climes –
> But general Homes
> Like Gnomes –
>
> Their Coming, may be known
> By Couriers within –
> Their going – is not –
> For they're never gone –

The unnamed hosts were not an invading army, but visitors, to be cordially received. If she felt herself haunted, the feeling only drove her to give expression to the thoughts that crowded upon her with their coming. It seems probable that at this point she seriously took up her role of poet, and began to work at her craft with full acceptance of her creative gift. Writing now to save her life, Emily was almost overwhelmed by the verses that poured from her pen. She knew now that, aside from its therapeutic value, the work for its own sake must go on.

In the great mass of poems in writing of about 1862 — one more than the number of days in the year — the prevailing atmosphere is that of pain. With only a few exceptions, the poems of love and the lover have to do with separation, renunciation, or a postponed reunion in heaven. In one of the best known,

> There came a Day at Summer's full,
> Entirely for me –

she recounts the climax of the story, making acknowledgment of a love that is not to be fulfilled. Of the lovers at the hour of parting she says:

> So faces on two Decks, look back,
> Bound to opposing lands –

and concludes:

> Sufficient troth, that we shall rise –
> Deposed – at length, the Grave –
> To that new Marriage,
> Justified – through Calvaries of Love –

In spite of the overwhelming sense of loss running through most of the poems at that time, there are others that speak of the lover as the life giver, and suggest the direction in which she will find healing. "To my small Hearth His fire came" tells how the coming of love brought illumination within. It is significant that the past tense is used throughout, showing that in looking back she was able to begin evaluating her experience.

In "I live with Him – I see His face," the spiritual union with the lover within the individual who loves brings the conviction that "Life like This – is stopless" and therefore the experience of love teaches immortality. Another poem, "He touched me, so I live to know," tells of the difference she finds in herself since being permitted, just once, to touch the loved one.

But the poem that expresses most fully the effect of love on the individual describes the call to full adulthood in terms of a second baptism.

> I'm ceded – I've stopped being Their's –
> The name They dropped upon my face
> With water, in the country church
> Is finished using, now,
> And They can put it with my Dolls,
> My childhood, and the string of spools,
> I've finished threading – too –
>
> Baptized, before, without the choice,
> But this time, consciously, of Grace –
> Unto supremest name –
> Called to my Full – The Crescent dropped –
> Existence's whole Arc, filled up,
> With one small Diadem.
>
> My second Rank – too small the first –
> Crowned – Crowing – on my Father's breast –

TO LIVE IS ENDOWMENT

A half unconscious Queen –
But this time – Adequate – Erect,
With Will to choose, or to reject,
And I choose, just a Crown –

The word "Crown," which appears in several poems, always implies an honor conferred, and dedication to the one who conferred it. Yet, despite this vision of the call to fullness of life as an individual, Emily wrote during the same period an expression of her feeling of complete identity with the loved one.

Empty my Heart, of Thee –
It's single Artery –
Begin, and leave Thee out –
Simply Extinction's Date –

Much Billow hath the Sea –
One Baltic – They –
Subtract Thyself, in play,
And not enough of me
Is left – to put away –
"Myself" meant Thee –

Erase the Root – no Tree –
Thee – then – no me –
The Heavens stripped –
Eternity's vast pocket, picked –

The theme is similar to that in the desperate poem of the previous year, "If *He dissolve* – then – there is *nothing – more*," but this time there is a marked advance, both in poetic quality and in emotional control. It is a statement made in philosophic calm, not the cry of a lost child in the dark.

Emily was now able to look at herself, to recall her experience and record her sensations in passing through the crisis of suffering. She had moods of resentment at having been stirred out of her unconscious state, as expressed in

> Of Course – I prayed –
> And did God Care?
> He cared as much as on the Air
> A Bird – had stamped her foot –
> And cried "Give Me" –
> My Reason – Life –
> I had not had – but for Yourself –
> 'Twere better Charity
> To leave me in the Atom's Tomb –
> Merry, and Nought, and gay, and numb –
> Than this smart Misery.

There were sensations of numbness and periods of dreaming, indulged in because it is easier to believe the experience is a dream than to wake and find it is reality. Most of all there was the illusion of death, and the sensation of nonexistence in chaos. It is hard to imagine a more devastating picture of negativity than is found in the following poem, even though it is expressed in terms of the senses.

> It was not Death, for I stood up,
> And all the Dead, lie down –
> It was not Night, for all the Bells
> Put out their Tongues, for Noon.
>
> It was not Frost, for on my Flesh
> I felt Siroccos – crawl –
> Nor Fire – for just my Marble feet
> Could keep a Chancel, cool –
>
> And yet it tasted, like them all,
> The Figures I have seen

TO LIVE IS ENDOWMENT

Set orderly, for Burial,
Reminded me, of mine –

As if my life were shaven,
And fitted to a frame,
And could not breathe without a key,
And 'twas like Midnight, some –

When everything that ticked – has stopped –
And Space stares all around –
Or Grisly frosts – first Autumn morns,
Repeal the Beating Ground –

But, most, like Chaos – Stopless – cool –
Without a Chance, or Spar –
Or even a Report of Land –
To justify – Despair.

Striking as these images evoked by the sensations are, they do
not stir the reader as deeply as those in another poem written
with the poet's intuition, which took her beyond the purely
personal aspect of experience. In an extraordinary abstraction
of the ultimate extremity of loneliness, she found, not mean-
ingless chaos, but a vision of the great wholeness of the universe, expressed in the word "Circumference."

I saw no Way – The Heavens were stitched –
I felt the Columns close –
The Earth reversed her Hemispheres –
I touched the Universe –

And back it slid – and I alone –
A Speck upon a Ball –
Went out upon Circumference –
Beyond the Dip of Bell –

By living her own experience through to the utmost she

passed the limits of the purely personal, and touched something vastly larger. The change from the personal to the suprapersonal goal is illustrated in two letters written three years apart. In 1859 she wrote to Dr. and Mrs. Holland, "*My business is to love.*" In her letter to Higginson of July 1862 she said, "My business is circumference."

While this inner struggle was going on, the creative power of the poet was expending itself with the force of a cataract, and she was writing voluminously on life and death, nature and people. At the same time she carried on the ordinary tasks and the social relations that were demanded of her.

> I tie my Hat – I crease my Shawl –
> Life's little duties do – precisely –

she wrote, ending the poem with the explanation that such behavior in time of stress is "To hold our Senses – on." But unconscious forces were at work beneath the safe realm of "sense," and a few poems contain images from so deep a level that she may not have understood them herself.

In a poem with the quality of a dream the theme of treasure to be found under the sea appeared. It was not the first time Emily had used this image, for in 1861, when the state of being in love was most intense, she wrote four stanzas, beginning "*One Life* of so much Consequence," in which she stated the worth of the man she loved. The second stanza reads:

> *One Pearl* – to me – so signal –
> That I would instant dive –
> Although – I *knew* – to *take* it –
> Would *cost* me – *just a life!*

The pearl is used as only one of several ways of estimating the value of the person whom she names in the final lines a "Monarch," and the sea where it is hidden exists only as a means of proving that the fulfillment of her love is worth the sacrifice of life itself. After the blow had fallen, and she was staggering to her feet on shaky ground, she wrote again of the pearl, but with quite different significance. It clarifies the terms in which the poem is expressed to recall the lines from Browning's *Paracelsus,* which Emily had undoubtedly read, using similar imagery.

> Are there not, Festus, are there not, dear Michal,
> Two points in the adventure of the diver,
> One — when, a beggar, he prepares to plunge,
> One — when, a prince, he rises with his pearl?
> Festus, I plunge!

Twisting the sequence of Browning's thought, she wrote,

> The Malay – took the Pearl –
> Not – I – the Earl –
> I – feared the Sea – too much
> Unsanctified – to touch –
>
> Praying that I might be
> Worthy – the Destiny –
> The Swarthy fellow swam –
> And bore my Jewel – Home –

This is not a figure of speech — it is live drama, acted between herself and a seemingly irrelevant figure brought up from the depths of her own mind. The poem concludes:

> Home to the Hut! What lot
> Had I – the Jewel – got –

Borne on a Dusky Breast –
I had not deemed a Vest
Of Amber – fit –

The Negro never knew
I – wooed it – too –
To gain, or be undone –
Alike to Him – One –

The image of the dangerous sea is used here with new
meaning, for she has come to recognize that in the depths
she feared lies the treasure that is rightfully hers. The pearl
is not only a jewel for which a great price may be paid, but
its spherical form represents the wholeness that Emily was
reaching for. But, at the time when this dream or fantasy
came to her, her conscious, superior self was defrauded of
the pearl because of her fear of the unknown and a sense of
unworthiness that was part of the religious conflict from
which she had suffered since her adolescent years. The figure
of the Malay who seizes it, a primitive unconscious being
whom she feels to be greatly inferior, is the dark reverse side
of her own psychic image of man, the opposite of the bright
guiding figure seen in the lover, in whose light she had been
lifted to new levels. The primitive human being, at one with
himself and the world of nature, simply lives, unaware of the
value of the pearl he possesses. To gain the treasure the
superior being must recognize the Malay in himself, and
humbly accept his services as a diver.

There is no record of any further dreams or fantasies that
carried on the theme of the treasure, and if Emily won the
pearl of wholeness in the end it was not by retrieving it from

the Malay. Two other poems of this time have to do with the life of the instincts, but only to acknowledge that something has been lost. In one she revives the leopard image she had used when, in the first flush of love, her whole being had been flooded with new life. This time, associating the leopard with something vital in herself for which she can find no place in the social pattern, she pleads for pity and understanding of the wild creature in an alien environment.

> Civilization – spurns – the Leopard!
> Was the Leopard – bold?
> Deserts – never rebuked her Satin –
> Ethiop – her Gold –
> Tawny – her Customs –
> She was Conscious –
> Spotted – her Dun Gown –
> This was the Leopard's nature – Signor –
> Need – a keeper – frown?
>
> Pity – the Pard – that left her Asia –
> Memories – of Palm –
> Cannot be stifled – with Narcotic –
> Nor suppressed – with Balm –

Another dreamlike poem of a particularly eerie quality, made stronger by the manner of simple statement in which it is written, uses a tiger instead of a leopard as its subject.

> A Dying Tiger – moaned for Drink –
> I hunted all the Sand –
> I caught the Dripping of a Rock
> And bore it in my Hand –
>
> His Mighty Balls – in death were thick –
> But searching – I could see

64

OURSELF BEHIND OURSELF

A Vision on the Retina
Of Water – and of me –

'Twas not my blame – who sped too slow –
'Twas not his blame – who died
While I was reaching him –
But 'twas – the fact that He was dead –

The writer feels no fear of the dangerous beast — only pity for him in his extremity. She remains curiously remote from the tiger, which was the creature of her own unconscious mind. She simply recognizes the fact that it was his fate to die, and she could do nothing to prevent it. Her sole connection with him is in the image on his eyeballs — herself with the life-giving water that came too late. One is reminded of the custom of the Brahmans, who, it is said, send their sons alone and unarmed into the jungle at night, that they may meet a tiger eye to eye, and in conquering their fear learn to know and control the tiger in themselves. Emily recognized herself in the dying eyes of the tiger, but her life had passed the point at which his power could be realized in her.

After a great storm, the wind, though shifting to another quarter, does not subside at once, and the process of reconstruction must be started in shelterless desolation. For Emily it must have seemed as if all had been swept away in a flood and she was left alone to rebuild her house little by little. She had let go the outgrown attitudes she had held before her awakening, and the revelation that had come through love had been projected into the person of the one she loved. She had failed to claim from the unconscious the "pearl of great price," because of her fear of what the deep waters might contain. The great life force that was in the beast of the jungle had died before she could reach it with her small offering of succoring water. Whence, then, was to come the power to begin again?

In Emily's groping progress toward a philosophy on which to build, one of the first signs of a positive trend appeared in a little poem, a triumph of condensation and control. Later she was to find it so important that she revised it twice, at intervals of several years. I give it in the first version, that of 1862.

> When I hoped – I feared –
> Since – I hoped – I dared
> Everywhere – alone –
> As a Church – remain.
>
> Ghost – may not alarm –
> Serpent – may not charm –
> He is King of Harm –
> Who hath suffered Him –

Since I stopped hoping, she is saying, I have also ceased to fear. Acceptance of fate frees one from the conflicting pulls of hope and fear, which are inseparable. One who has lived through the worst is released from the power of harm. On the solid rock of accepted fact a footing can be found from which a more positive step can be taken.

Many of the poems written during the years immediately following 1862 are of a new character. The struggle is still intense, but the pain and passion have given way to a concentration of the whole being on the effort of affirmation.

"Who am I?" she seems to be saying, "What can I find in my own mind and soul on which to build a new life?" The exploration demanded courage. She had already said in 1862:

> One need not be a Chamber – to be Haunted –
> One need not be a House –
> The Brain – has Corridors surpassing
> Material Place –
>
> Far safer of a Midnight – meeting
> External Ghost –
> Than an Interior – Confronting –
> That cooler – Host.
>
> Far safer, through an Abbey – gallop –
> The Stones a'chase –
> Than Moonless – One's A'self encounter –
> In lonesome place –
>
> Ourself – behind Ourself – Concealed –
> Should startle – most –
> Assassin – hid in our Apartment –
> Be Horror's least –
>
> The Prudent – carries a Revolver –
> He bolts the Door –
> O'erlooking a Superior Spectre –
> More near –

In the dim corridors of the mind one can prepare to meet and defend oneself from objective fears, but the greatest horror to be encountered is the sudden consciousness of the hidden self, as close as one's own shadow, yet charged with ghostly power. Added to the draft of the poem are two alternative readings for the closing lines that help to explain the effect of terrifying surprise in the spectral meeting. These are:

TO LIVE IS ENDOWMENT

> A Spectre – infinite – accompanying –
> He fails to fear –

and

> Maintaining a Superior Spectre –
> None saw –

The horror is strengthened by the fact that the ego has remained unconscious and unafraid until the revelation occurs.

A poem written the following year repeats the theme in different terms, carrying the thought a step further.

> The Loneliness One dare not sound –
> And would as soon surmise
> As in it's Grave go plumbing
> To ascertain the size –
> The Loneliness whose worst alarm
> Is lest itself should see –
> And perish from before itself
> For just a scrutiny –
>
> The Horror not to be surveyed –
> But skirted in the Dark –
> With Consciousness suspended –
> And Being under Lock –
>
> I fear me this – is Loneliness –
> The Maker of the soul
> It's Caverns and it's Corridors
> Illuminate – or seal –

The horror is still present, and the fear of the dark can only be alleviated by bringing in the light of God. Without the illumination the only course is to seal up the caverns and corridors of the soul and never enter them.

The poems fail to tell us the shape of the specters that so

terrified the writer, but the implication is that she sought the illumination of God in which to look at them. The verses that grew out of her scrutiny were not descriptive, but were rather the crystallization of her thought after the specters had been met and dealt with. A very important poem of this period is the following, which brings out a new attitude toward the object of her love.

> You constituted Time –
> I deemed Eternity
> A Revelation of Yourself –
> 'Twas therefore Deity
>
> The Absolute – removed
> The Relative away –
> That I unto Himself adjust
> My slow idolatry –

Emily had begun to stand apart from her experience, to separate the person loved from the projections made to him, and to find a reason for the loss she still felt as the supreme fact in her life. She carried the thought further, though without personal application, in an analysis of the act of renunciation.

> Renunciation – is a piercing Virtue –
> The letting go
> A Presence – for an Expectation –
> Not now –
> The putting out of Eyes –
> Just Sunrise –
> Lest Day –
> Day's Great Progenitor –
> Outvie
> Renunciation – is the Choosing

TO LIVE IS ENDOWMENT

Against itself –
Itself to justify
Unto itself –
When larger function –
Make that appear –
Smaller – that Covered Vision – Here –

In the past Emily had used "Day" as the image of the illumination love brought her. At that time it was the summation of life for her — it "covered" her "vision" completely. Now she had found a still "larger function," using that word perhaps in the mathematical sense, meaning related values. She saw the generating power of God behind the appearance of the light of day, and let go the immediate joy for the expectation of a greater experience.

It was not that she had ceased to hold the attitude of devotion and consecration to the love that had engulfed her, but that power had actually gone from it into her life, to be used in other ways. Jung has said that the difference between the image of woman in man and the image of man in woman is that the former represents the man's soul, while the latter represents the woman's mind. This seems to be borne out by the nature of the poems that form a large proportion of those Emily wrote in the years 1863–65. Among those written in 1863, more than a third are philosophical, and many of these are in the form of definitions, such as the one above on renunciation. The first lines of some actually use the phraseology of the text books, beginning "Remorse – is," "The Spirit is," "The Truth – is," "Grief is." As the past was translated from the terms of emotion into those of mind, she was framing her new structure with precision. Whether or not she actually felt at this time such solidarity of conviction as she expressed in the following poem on the self, she could at least see psychic integrity as a goal.

> On a Columnar Self –
> How ample to rely
> In Tumult – or Extremity –
> How good the Certainty
>
> That Lever cannot pry –
> And Wedge cannot divide
> Conviction – That Granitic Base –
> Though None be on our Side –
>
> Suffice Us – for a Crowd –
> Ourself – and Rectitude –
> And that Assembly – not far off
> From furthest Spirit – God –

At the very time when Emily was working out her philosophy, she was also establishing her habits of withdrawal from the world around her. In 1863 her chosen way of life had become so apparent that her family and friends were troubled by it. They felt that she was dramatizing her situation, and should not be encouraged to indulge a tendency that to them undoubtedly appeared morbid.

It is indeed hard to reconcile the contradiction between the courageous and positive trend of her thinking at this time and her inclination to shrink from all contact with the outside world, unless one remembers that the main result of the inner experience had been the attainment of full maturity as a poet. To a woman who was not an artist, such psychic events as she had undergone would have led to a quite different adjustment. But an artist of such power and sensitivity as Emily Dickinson, however "columnar" her self might be, was not free to live as others. Something had to be sacrificed. In her case it was the outer shell, the protective covering usually built up from the individual's assumptions about life and the habits, traditional and personal, that govern his behavior in social situations. These Emily had put aside as inessential, and, since she was not forced by outer circumstances to deal directly with the demands of society, her natural bent was encouraged. She lived so close to the center of her being, to the mainsprings of the life of spirit, that she brought to every contact an emotional charge and an enhanced awareness that made extraordinary demands on her store of vital energy. She carried with her into every least happening in daily life the whole sum of her consciousness, and, since her consciousness covered a far broader field than that of the average person, every aspect of nature and every human situation was invested with the power to evoke a deep response. It is no wonder, then, that she felt the need of limiting her sources of stimulus. A way of living that began as a necessity in a period of great stress continued as the habit of a lifetime, to the bafflement even of her friends, who could not fully understand that within her chosen limits her life was crowded with rich and varied experience.

Emily's dedication to the absent lover was not at once relinquished when she began to find her footing on a new level, but it was undergoing a change. Love is not lost: it is transformed. When the man she loved is withdrawn, a woman must redeem from her love the power and meaning it held for her, or she will be possessed by a ghostly lover whose hold prevents her from moving forward into a new phase. Now, no longer contained in the loved one, Emily had drawn from her love the masculine element that set her mind free, and had translated into art the varied emotional states that had swept through her being. Yet, to her, as to other women, it was natural to direct her living toward the person whom she loved, even if he had receded into a disembodied existence. She recognized this need when she wrote in 1862,

> I tend my flowers for thee –
> Bright Absentee!

For a time she still needed the focal point found in the lover to whom she had dedicated her life, and with whom she looked forward to reunion in heaven. Reunion on earth would, after all, have made demands on her that she could not meet, for the lover was now wholly spiritual, a companion of the soul to whom she could act her life.

In the poems that complete the cycle two trends emerge. One follows the old pattern of personal devotion, of longing and waiting for the fulfillment of love in another sphere. The other shows a change in the character of the spiritual relation to the symbolic figure with whom the loved one had been identified. In the time of greatest stress, Emily had written a poem of total dedication to a man she could not marry.

> Title divine – is mine!
> The Wife – without the Sign!

TO LIVE IS ENDOWMENT

Acute Degree – conferred on me –
Empress of Calvary!
Royal – all but the Crown!
Betrothed – without the swoon
God sends us Women –
When you – hold – Garnet to Garnet –
Gold – to Gold –
Born – Bridalled – Shrouded –
In a Day –
"My Husband" – women say –
Stroking the Melody –
Is *this* – the way?

Here her story is completely dramatized. The lines,

Born – Bridalled – Shrouded –
In a Day –

contain the whole experience of life and death, and her suffering is transmuted into spiritual ecstasy. From the marriage in heaven she now passes to the role of a nun, who becomes the bride of Christ. In a poem written in 1864, the human lover has disappeared, her earthly fate is fully accepted, and the transfer of allegiance from the relative to the absolute, foreshadowed in "You constituted Time," has been accomplished.

Given in Marriage unto Thee
Oh thou Celestial Host –
Bride of the Father and the Son
Bride of the Holy Ghost.

Other Betrothal shall dissolve –
Wedlock of Will, decay –
Only the Keeper of this Ring
Conquer Mortality –

Although a number of poems about her experience of love were still to come, they were written in reminiscent vein, and the lover was no longer to carry the full weight of her soul. In fact, she had come to perceive that he existed within herself, and that her mind was free to exercise the power to heighten or diminish his importance.

> I make His Crescent fill or lack –
> His Nature is at Full
> Or Quarter – as I signify –
> His Tides – do I control –
>
> He holds superior in the Sky
> Or gropes, at my Command
> Behind inferior Clouds – or round
> A Mist's slow Colonnade –
>
> But since We hold a Mutual Disc –
> And front a Mutual Day –
> Which is the Despot, neither knows –
> Nor Whose – the Tyranny –

The poem is sufficiently obscure to allow several interpretations. It has usually been understood as an acknowledgment of woman's power over an actual lover, or a fantasy of longing for such a condition. It could also be understood in a religious sense, as a statement of the importance of faith, which according to the degree of its intensity enlarges or lessens the individual's conception of God. The moon image, however, seems hardly appropriate even to an unconventional picture of the Christian God, but quite in keeping with the ancient myths whose rituals were sacred to women. Emily had already used the image of the moon in the sense of the soul's lover in an earlier poem, "The Moon is distant from the Sea." Then it was the lover who controlled the tides, and she who responded obediently to his commands. Now the situation has been reversed; the lover is no longer a human being, but a part of herself. The perfect circle of the moon's face, held between them in mutual accord, is the symbol of the union.

Since life is never without motion and change, and human documents are at best approximations of the truth, many questions remain, but one thing stands out clearly. After six years of intense creativity, Emily Dickinson the poet had completed the greater part of her life's work, but Emily Dickinson the woman — a white-gowned mystery to strangers, a many-faceted, glowing personality to those who knew her — was just entering her years of maturity. Her dedication was no longer to be to the memory of a man she had loved, or to the hope of spiritual reunion with him in the future life, but to that inner integrity of soul that can only be described through the use of symbols. In her own words, it is the "pearl," the "kernel," the "flower of the soul"; when projected into life and beyond life it is the "disc" and above all "circumference." In 1865, at the end of the creative period, she wrote of the change that had taken place:

> I heard, as if I had no Ear
> Until a Vital Word
> Came all the way from Life to me
> And then I knew I heard.

> I saw, as if my Eye were on
> Another, till a Thing
> And now I know 'twas Light, because
> It fitted them, came in.

OURSELF BEHIND OURSELF

I dwelt, as if Myself were out,
My Body but within
Until a Might detected me
And set my kernel in.

And Spirit turned unto the Dust
"Old Friend, thou knowest me,"
And Time went out to tell the News
And met Eternity

THE FINEST SECRET

Emotional currents in the life of
Emily Dickinson after 1865

Every child knows the value of a secret. For Emily Dickinson secrets never lost their fascination, and she was able to share the child's pleasure, not only in knowing something that was his alone to enjoy, but the equally alluring power to reveal to another person what he knew. In a poem beginning, "Our little secrets slink away," she spoke of "the niggardly delight / To make each other stare." This crude satisfaction, however, was the most trivial of the emotions evoked by secrets, for at the opposite extreme she recognized with awe the explosive power contained in hidden knowledge. In 1862 she wrote:

> A Secret told –
> Ceases to be a Secret – then –
> A Secret – kept –
> That – can appal but One –
>
> Better of it – continual be afraid –
> Than it –
> And Whom you told it to – beside –

Above the personal level lay her frequent use of the word to express the mysteries inherent in human life and in man's relation to the infinite. Carrying with her always this high sense of mystery, she sometimes invested ordinary acts with a dramatic atmosphere.

After a visit from Mrs. Holland in October 1870, Emily felt it necessary to explain to her friend why she had tried, apparently without success, to draw her away from the family group for a private interview.

> Perhaps you thought dear Sister, I wanted to elope with you and feared a vicious Father.
> It was not quite that. . . .
> Life is the finest secret.
> So long as that remains, we must all whisper.
> With that sublime exception I had no clandestineness.

The nature of life itself was her excuse. Its content was secret — unknown, in large part, to the involuntary bearers of it. The most one could do, she felt, was to share the knowledge of its secrecy reverently, lest we break the spell under which we live. If the meaning remained obscure, the emotional response to being alive was enough to bring a sense of supreme value into daily living.

When Thomas Wentworth Higginson had called on her, shortly before Mrs. Holland's visit, her life appeared to him so restricted as to stifle the vital forces, and he was amazed to hear her say, "I find ecstasy in living — the mere sense of living is joy enough." "Ecstasy" is a strong word, but Emily Dickinson chose her words with a poet's perception, and was fully aware of their power. She used the word many times in her poems, sometimes attributing the emotion, especially in the earlier poems, to the singing bird and the butterfly in flight, but finding it also in the agonized leap of a dying deer. To the human soul it came as an inner condition of unreasoning joy in moments of sudden revelation of a spiritual nature.

Emily's emphatic expressions about life were uttered at a time when she was just emerging from a period of withdrawal lasting several years. From 1866 to 1870 there is little to indicate, either in the occasional poems or the few letters, a particular trend of thought or a special emotional drift, and the meaning of the blank interval can only be found in the effects seen at its close.

One unfinished poem, however, written about 1867 — a year to which only ten poems and one letter have been attributed — suggests the attitude she held toward her own way of life at the time. It is a rough worksheet, containing alternate words and lines, and seems never to have passed beyond the form in which she jotted it down under some compulsion to explain herself to herself.

> I fit for them —
> I seek the Dark
> Till I am thorough fit.
> The labor is a sober one
> With the austerer sweet – an – this
> With this sufficient sweet
> That abstinence of mine produce
> A purer food for them, if I succeed,
> If not I had
> The transport of the Aim —

The first line, made obscure by the omission of "myself" after "fit," and curiously awkward in its sound, may be read as a concise statement of the thought carried out in the succeeding lines. It answers her inner questioning as to her real motive in avoiding contact with the outside world. There are signs of a conscious struggle between the demands of her small circle and her own deep need for replenishment from a source unknown to the others. She loved her friends, but she must protect herself from the subtle draining of power that their society brought her. It is possible that her aim was not wholly personal, but that she was thinking of herself as a poet when she spoke of the "purer food" she hoped to bring them as a result of her withdrawal. Her instinct was to follow the way of nature, which lets the seed lie dormant until conditions are right for its growth toward the sun. Resting after the long and intense experience of spiritual death and rebirth that came with the period of her greatest creativity in the early 1860's, she was feeling her way toward the establishment of a frame into which her life could fit, and where she could be most herself.

There was no distinct beginning or ending to this period of withdrawal, for the habit of seclusion came gradually and was never again broken. The poems and letters of the last twenty years, however, show that life did not stop for her when she closed the door, but passed through as many phases as appear in the lives of those whose experience is in the active world of men and women. When she wrote to Mrs. Holland in 1870, "Life is the finest secret," the plant she had cherished in darkness was pushing with vigor into the light.

Since her letters became her chief means of expression as the years went on, it is through them that one can best trace the development of her life within its self-imposed limits. One cannot rely on the memories of the few who saw her, for they were colored by their own views and limited by the kind of experience they shared with her. Her elusiveness, her charm, her wit, and her delight in the spontaneity of childhood, which have taken a prominent place in all descriptions of her, give only the outer aspects of the personality that beguiled and mystified her friends. The stark power of her thoughts amazed but seemingly repelled the feminist Higginson. Her niece and nephews and their young friends found in her an ally who belonged neither to their own world nor to that of their parents, and whose mind stimulated their imaginations. Her devoted sister Lavinia saw her as a precious companion, close and dear as life itself, but something apart, to be cherished and protected along with the silver service and the fine china. It is doubtful whether her sister-in-law, Sue, whose independent intelligence and expansive nature had given her in earlier years the role of confidante and critic in matters of the mind and heart, had ever really shared Emily's point of view enough to understand the path she had chosen. During the years of seclusion, she seems to have become to Sue a quaint relic of the ardent companion of the past, occasionally sending out from her retreat glowing words with which the guests next door could be regaled.

Even in Emily's own words, as found in the occasional poems and numerous letters of her last sixteen years, it is by no means easy to find the basic pattern, for a letter is written in relation to a particular person. Her letters to her younger cousins, the Norcross sisters, full as they are of an easy play of elder-sister affection, reflect chiefly her view of the matters of daily living that are of interest to members of the same family. The circumstances under which the many little notes to Sue were written are hidden from us, so that the philosophical character they often show is left suspended, without application. The freedom and warmth with which she wrote to Mrs. Holland imply a background of mutual understanding in matters of the main issues and motives that underlie the events of life, yet there remains a certain reticence in regard to her own inner world. The few letters she wrote to Samuel Bowles after 1870 are mainly ejaculations of gratitude to a man in whose company she always found delight, and who returned her deep admiration with affectionate sympathy. To Higginson, whom she saw only twice, she gave more of her mind, but toward him she maintained to the end the attitude — one might almost say the pose — of pupil to teacher. In the many gemlike notes to neighbors, written for the most part to fit an occasion in their lives and directed wholly to that end, she withheld her own life as carefully as she withheld her physical presence from the eyes of Amherst.

Although no one series or group of letters can provide a picture of what Emily Dickinson's life meant to her, the whole collection, read in its approximately chronological order, does provide a living source from which such a picture can be drawn. It is not so much to direct expression of thought or feeling, however, as to changes of style, choice of words, shifts of emphasis in the modes of expression that we must look for indications of where the emotional foundations lie and how they alter and develop as the steady flow of psychic energy carries her forward.

Emily was speaking of herself as a poet when she quoted in a letter to Higginson in 1866 a poem she had first drafted several years before, but the meaning she wished to convey was equally applicable to her personal life.

> Except the smaller size
> No lives are round –
> These – hurry to a sphere
> And show and end –
> The larger – slower grow
> And later hang –
> The Summers of Hesperides
> Are long.

The custom of the time, the economic position of her family, the character of her father as its dominating member, and her own need for outer security all combined to carry her into middle age without forcing her to take on the fundamental responsibilities of everyday life. Mr. Dickinson not only provided a comfortable living for his wife and daughters, but warded off the assaults of the outside world for the one who chose to live vertically within the safety of his home rather than horizontally in a wider field. She had his protection as long as he lived, and under it she could develop her own outlook in perfect security. That she endured the torture of inner revolution during the critical years that made her a poet, while still revolving in the daily round of the small women's world of which Edward Dickinson was the axis, speaks not only for the spiritual stamina she inherited from her Puritan forebears, but for the freedom her father gave her to be herself.

Sharing her father's independence of mind, though it appeared in a wholly new pattern, she relied on his invincibility while she could smile at his foibles. During the years of re-adjustment, of which he probably knew little, she rested behind the defenses he had erected for her as one of the primary concerns of a man with a family. She filled the place of daughter as unconditionally as her father functioned in his own role, making his bread and giving him her companionship when he wished it, thus bringing a balance to the relation. When she wrote to Mrs. Holland, just a year before Mr. Dickinson died, "I was thinking of thanking you for the kindness to Vinnie. She has no Father and Mother but me and I have no Parents but her," she was indicating the remoteness she and her sister felt from their parents in matters touching their hearts. In a different area of their life, however, the father's place was as real as the sun in the sky, and was so completely accepted that it need not be thought of. She certainly was not aware that her tie to him was in any way inappropriate in a woman of forty-two. As long as his protective presence remained, she continued to live in the enclosed freedom it provided.

After the largely unrecorded years of the late 1860's a sudden expansion marks the beginning of a new period in Emily Dickinson's correspondence. The increase in the number of letters was partly due to external reasons, such as the return of the Hollands after two years in Europe and the stimulus given to her friendship with Higginson by her first meeting with him. Aside from this, an inner change is suggested by a new trend that is noticeable in the letters themselves, not only in content but in form and appearance. The handwriting becomes larger and bolder, the paragraphs are shorter, often consisting of only a few words, and an aphoristic style develops, as if she were experimenting with new prose forms. Each statement becomes emphatic. Whatever the subject, the main theme is Life — with a capital L — Life of which she is a part, which she sees in everything around her, but which she sees in perspective and in general terms rather than in particularities.

"Life is the finest secret" is followed during the next few years by such statements as the one with which she began a letter to Higginson in 1872: "To live is so startling, it leaves but little room for other occupations." To Louise and Frances Norcross she wrote in 1873, "Life is a spell so exquisite that everything conspires to break it," and to Mrs. Holland in the same year, "To live is Endowment. It puts me in mind of that singular Verse in the Revelations — 'Every several Gate was of one Pearl.' " In the protected world of her home, where her separateness was respected, she was able to observe life as if it were a mountain seen from the air. What she saw prompted such pronouncements as these, which she sent in little notes to Sue: "Oh Matchless Earth — We underrate the chance to dwell in Thee," and "We meet no Stranger but Ourself," and, in the letters to Higginson and Mrs. Holland — her principal correspondents at the time — "Even the Possible has it's insoluble particle," and "Each expiring Secret leaves an Heir, distracting still." Every small happening of daily life was fitted into the pattern of the great whole of which she was ever conscious, the infinite mystery of life and death.

There was a sharp increase in the number of poems that, according to the present chronology, may be credited to the years 1870–1874, with fifty written in 1873. This was not only the largest number in any year since 1865, but a larger number than she was to write in any succeeding year. There are few among them of such emotional intensity as is felt in many of those that were distilled from the ecstasy and pain of the years of her awakening as a woman and a poet. She was no longer writing to save her life, but was using her gift with maturer insight as a means of expression for the stimulations of mind and soul that came as the steady accompaniment of daily living. There are many poems of nature, poems about people, and philosophical observations. There are several poems of recollection and a few that seem specifically autobiographical. One of these, written in 1871, is indicative of the tone of the period:

> I should not dare to be so sad
> So many Years again –
> A Load is first impossible
> When we have put it down –
>
> The Superhuman then withdraws
> And we who never saw
> The Giant at the other side
> Begin to perish now.

The past has been assimilated, the terms it imposed accepted, and the way opened for a new relation to life, less acutely personal and more expansive in scope.

These were probably the least troubled years of Emily's life and her letters reflect many interests. There are frequent references to books, especially in the letters to Higginson, whom she considered her principal authority on literature in spite of her failure to agree with him on some of the authors he recommended. She read Darwin and the magazine articles that discussed his theories, speculating on the scientific thought of her day in relation to the values she cherished. There were friends to enjoy, for although she no longer went out to meet them there were always chosen spirits whom she welcomed within her own walls. She shared with her family a warm and growing friendship with the Reverend and Mrs. Jonathan L. Jenkins and their children, who were playmates of her own nephew and niece. The glowing presence of Samuel Bowles, who never failed to call on her when he went to Amherst, gladdened and stimulated her more, perhaps, than the company of anyone else. She looked forward to the visits of Louise and Fanny Norcross, and maintained a warmly personal relation with Dr. and Mrs. Holland, though their visits became less frequent after they moved to New York in 1872. There were also visits from her father's friend, Judge Lord of Salem, and his wife — a couple whose affectionate interest was shared by all the members of the family. It is probable that she was corresponding regularly with Dr. Wadsworth, who had returned from San Francisco to Philadelphia, for in later references to him it is clear that she had been in constant touch with him for many years. During these years the pattern of her way of life seems to have expanded and developed outwardly as the inner growth demanded expression.

The sudden, complete, and irrevocable cessation of a powerful force leaves a terrifying void where it has been active. When, in June 1874, Edward Dickinson died alone in Boston after a collapse in the legislative hall, the shock was too great to be experienced all at once. The circumstances of his death, away from home and, as the family believed, with inadequate medical care, must have added much to the cruel pain of the blow.

In one sense, no one could have been better prepared than Emily for an encounter with sudden death. She had carried the burden of its mystery with her since adolescence, and, as Thomas Johnson points out, had "drawn it into the texture of five or six hundred poems," examining its effects on the dying and on those that were left. She had looked at her relation to her own death in several of its aspects, in poems of remarkable power and imagery. She had even admitted the possibility of her father's nearness to death three years earlier, when during his illness she wrote to Louise Norcross, "I think his physical life don't want to live any longer." But the actual effect of his sudden disappearance could not have been foreseen by the richest imagination. She wrote to the Norcrosses a few weeks after the event, "Though it is many nights, my mind never comes home," and in a letter to Higginson she spoke of "that Pause of Space which I call 'Father.'" To follow the dead in their adventure into a new dimension seems to be a universal human instinct. They leave us, but for a time we cannot leave them. As late as August 1876 Emily was writing to her Norcross cousins: "I dream about father every night, always a different dream, and forget what I am doing daytimes, wondering where he is. Without any body, I keep thinking. What kind can that be?"

Indeed, her letters show that for four years she was haunted by the thought of her father as she felt her way along in the strange new life of the house he had left. To Higginson in June 1877 she explained, "Since my Father's dying, everything sacred enlarged so – it was dim to own." And in January 1878 she wrote to her neighbor, Mrs. Hills: "It is a little more than three years since you tried to help us bid Father Good-Night, which was so impossible that it has never become less so."

It was not only the mystery of where her father had gone that filled her with awe and loneliness. After the first shock had passed her image of him had grown, as if his stature had become enhanced by removal. While he was alive she saw him in particulars. "Father steps like Cromwell when he gets the kindlings." When he was gone she began to see him as a whole, and was able to say, in grander perspective, "His Heart was pure and terrible and I think no other like it exists." As the person became separated from the parent in her recollection, she was able to speak of his lonely life and lonelier death with a tenderness of feeling that came from a certain detachment from the tie of a child to the father. At the same time his importance to her in another way seems to have grown. The father figure, disembodied, had sunk deep into the recesses of her mind, to appear as a living symbol in her dreams. "Always a different dream," she said, but gives us no light on the nature of the dreams, whose effect on her conscious preoccupation with the mystery of life after death must have been profound. It is only by tracing the changes in her outer life and their reflection in her letters that we can gather something of the meaning of the inner experience that brought them about.

Circumstances, of course, forced a change in the Dickinson family life. The main pillar was gone, and the structure must somehow be held up by those that were left. Austin took over the business affairs of his mother and sisters, who maintained during the first year a semblance at least of the character of the daily life they had pursued during Edward Dickinson's absences in Boston. Then Mrs. Dickinson, whose dependent nature and lack of physical stamina made adjustment almost impossible, suffered a stroke and became permanently incapable of carrying her share of the load. Lavinia shouldered the responsibility in relation to the outside world, but it is clear that Emily not only took part fully in the practical affairs of the house, as she had always done, but considered herself as the elder sister the head of the house. In offering help to Sue after her youngest child, Gilbert, was born in the summer of 1875, she assumed her authority when she wrote, "Emily and all that she has are at Sue's service, if of any comfort to Baby – Will send Maggie, if you will accept her." Six years later, in speaking of a new servant, she referred to herself as "Head of the Nation" of which he was the foot. It was a normal response to the challenge of circumstances, and it marked a step in her progress toward absorbing her father's power into her own life.

Surprisingly, as one reads the letters of the middle seventies there is a subtle sense of lessening of tension in the structure and style. No sharp lines can be drawn marked by definite dates, but certain tendencies are apparent. There are fewer aphorisms and abstractions. The approach is more direct, more related to the particular persons and circumstances with which she is concerned than with the thoughts they have evoked. In a letter to Mrs. Holland in 1877 she said, "The vitality of your syllables compensates for their infrequency. There is not so much Life as *talk* of Life, as a general thing." Although her own style had never lacked vital energy, her meaning is applicable to her own letters at this time, when a shift of emphasis brought her writing down to a more human level. The difference might be illustrated by two letters to Mrs. Holland, each written after a visit in Amherst. In 1873 Emily wrote:

Little Sister.
   I miss your childlike Voice –
   I miss your Heroism.
   I feel that I lose combinedly a Soldier and a Bird.
   I trust that you experience a trifling destitution.
   Thank you for having been.
   These timid Elixirs are obtained too seldom.

In 1877 her letter began:

   I miss my little Sanctuary and her redeeming ways. A Savior in a Nut, is sweeter to the grasp than ponderous Prospectives.
   Come again, and go not – which when a faithful invitation, is the sweetest known!

Reduced to the simplest terms, both letters say, "I miss you. Please come again," but the first uses images to build a work of art around the friend, who remains as untouchable as if she were encased in crystal. In the second the phrase "my little Sanctuary" brings the writer into immediate relation with the friend. There is a vast difference between an invitation so oblique as "These timid Elixirs are obtained too seldom," and the direct approach of the "faithful invitation" — "Come again, and go not," which sets up a warm current of feeling flowing between the two friends.

Emily was now more deeply enmeshed in the fabric of life than she had ever been while her father lived. Two new relationships began to grow which, with the curious illogicality that often characterizes reality, fulfilled a similar emotional need, though one involved an older person and the other a child. So far little has been said of Emily's mother, and indeed it is very easy to overlook the fact that she had a mother, so strangely colorless Mrs. Dickinson remains in the reader's imagination. Her portrait shows a face of gentle propriety with a deprecating smile. There are no contemporary accounts of her personality except the uncomfortably negative phrases Emily used in describing her to Colonel Higginson: "I never had a mother. I suppose a mother is one to whom you hurry when you are troubled," and "My Mother does not care for thought." We see her in the letters of Emily's earlier years as an anxious housewife often stricken with illnesses that forced her daughters to take over her duties. She sends eatables to sick neighbors and persons in need, and her coming in from a walk with a burr on her shawl is a matter for comment. After she became paralyzed Emily wrote Mrs. Holland, "Mother misses power to ramble to her Neighbors – and the stale inflation of the minor News." She seems the embodiment of country gentility, and one wonders how she could ever have felt at home in the company of her own husband and children with their strongly individual traits. It was, perhaps, inevitable that she should become helpless and reverse the relation to that of the child of her daughters. After her death Emily explained what had happened. "We were never intimate Mother and Children while she was our Mother," she wrote to Mrs. Holland, "but Mines in the same Ground meet by tunneling and when she became our Child, the Affection came." Lacking a strong, positive experience of the mother-child relationship when she was young, Emily was slow in developing her own mother instinct, but, when it came through life's strange reversal, she was able to look back and see that the two had lain "in the same Ground."

Emily not only devoted herself to the care of this elderly child, but extended the feeling that began to live in the new relation to others outside her home. The sudden increase in these years of the number of little notes to neighbors could not be wholly a matter of chance. Written at first, perhaps, on her mother's behalf, they came to be expressions of her own wish to share the significant events in the lives of those around her, many of whom she had never seen. It was a return after twenty years to a fuller participation in the life of the village, but on terms that she could control, since she now felt free and secure in the way of life her being had demanded.

While Mrs. Dickinson was living out her defeated days as a cherished invalid, a new life was beginning to grow in Austin's house next door. During the eight brief years of little Gilbert's life he carried an unusual load of emotional meaning for those closest to him in both houses. His parents were middle-aged when he was born — his mother forty-five and his father a year older. Their other children, Ned and Martha, were fourteen and nine, and if he had not been a particularly winning child he might have suffered as an unwanted member. It was a difficult family situation into which he came, for tensions resulting from temperamental differences had already caused fissures in the fabric of his parents' marriage, and put a strain on the relations between the two houses. It is probable, however, that his very existence brought a measure of peace to the atmosphere, and he seems to have developed as a healthy, intelligent, and sunny child. For two years after his birth he is not mentioned in Emily's letters, and one may suppose that she saw little of him until he was able to roam across the lawn and his endearing personality began to find expression in speech. When she began to write of his exploits the references were all to "Austin's Baby," not Susan's, implying that his father took special comfort in his company. "Vinnie rode last Twilight – with Austin and the Baby, but the latter cried for the Moon, which saddened their Trip." " 'Home – sweet Home' – Austin's Baby sings – 'there is no place like Home – 'tis too – over to Aunt Vinnie's.' " "Austin's Baby says when surprised by statements. – 'There's–*sumth*n–else–there's–*Bumbul*–Beese.' "

Emily's affection and admiration for Sue were sadly torn by her loyalty to Austin, and the joy this little boy brought into his father's life must have been a special relief to her heart. His presence was like fresh air in both houses, but even his own baby charm and his special dearness to his father cannot fully account for Emily's deep attachment to him. It was not only as an adoring aunt that she sent a photograph of him in a letter to Helen Hunt Jackson when he was three years old. It is unfortunate that the letter itself is missing, but its purpose is explained in Mrs. Jackson's reply, which begins: "My face was not 'averted' in the least. It was only that I did not speak." In the final paragraph she says: "I send back the little baby face to tell you that I had not 'averted' my face — only the habit of speaking. It is an earnest and good little face: your brother's child I presume." Emily, fearing she had been forgotten, had sent Gilbert to plead for her, and Mrs. Jackson, deeming his mission unnecessary, used him again as a messenger of reassurance, to speak for her in honest simplicity.

Emily was never possessive in her attachment to Gilbert, for the child's individuality was deeply respected, yet he seemed in a sense peculiarly hers, with a kinship that had its roots in the figure of the eternal child, the symbol of rebirth. Life, which constantly renews itself, had brought her through another cycle in the death of her father and the dependence of her mother, and ushered her into a new phase of her own being.

Anyone who carefully examines the life and mind of Emily Dickinson is constantly checked in making statements about her by the appearance of the opposite characteristic to the one just noted. The fascination of her character is enhanced by paradoxes that continually baffle the observer. She had an extraordinary capacity for love and friendship, yet she shunned society. She was so absorbed in the spiritual world as to seem too ethereal for daily life, yet she could be as earthy as the bread, cakes, and puddings she made, and could turn instantly from a preoccupation with infinity to a playful and pithy humor. Full of tender sympathy for anyone she knew who was wronged, she could be merciless in her characterizations and was highly intolerant of stupidity. Although she was intensely concerned with the larger movements of life as they affected people she knew, she was seemingly unmoved by the predicaments of society in general. Her fear of contact with strangers was matched by the boldness of her thought, and her physical frailty by a vigor of spirit she could scarcely control. Perhaps the secret of her contradictions lay in the fact that she lived always so close to her own center that she maintained a tension between the opposites that left her free from domination by either side. If one is tempted by her failure to meet the world on its own terms to label her a neurotic, she suddenly blows away all categories by a revelation of how superbly she lived all that was vital within her chosen limits, never shirking or failing to meet whatever experience came to her in all its implications.

Opposites played an important part in her life, not only within herself but in the circumstances that affected her. The times of greatest vitality, when there was an upsurge of powerful emotions, provided the most violent contrasts of light and dark, joy and pain. Such was the case in the year 1878. The dullness of days spent in caring for her gentle but dependent invalid were relieved by the delight of surprises afforded by the budding personality of the little boy next door. At the same time a poignant grief had come in the death of Samuel Bowles at the beginning of the year. Although she felt herself to be "strongly built" emotionally and able to meet the face of sorrow, the loss of this intensely admired friend not only hurt her deeply, but brought once more to the surface the unanswered questions of the meaning of death and the hope of immortality. In almost every letter of the time and in a number of the poems, these questions recur. Her feeling demanded that she reach out to those who were closest to the friend she had lost. She poured out her sympathy to Mrs. Bowles, on whose friendship she had long ceased to count. She also opened her heart to Maria Whitney, a cousin of Mrs. Bowles who had been much with the family, and whose congenial companionship with her husband had not always been pleasing to the wife. She was living in a world of uncertainty and pain, but of strong and deep emotion that in itself gave meaning to life. It was at this time, when all the avenues of her feeling were wide open, that a wholly new experience began to take place.

It was natural that the two sisters, Emily and Lavinia, should have turned after their father's death to his most trusted friend for comfort and counsel. Judge Otis Phillips Lord is the only man who has been spoken of as an intimate friend of Edward Dickinson's, and it is probable that no one else came so close to that "pure and terrible" heart. Political and legal associates, neighbors and members of the Amherst College faculty deeply respected Mr. Dickinson, but few saw him in any but the particular aspect in which they happened to have relations with him. Lord, who had been a student at Amherst in the early years of the Dickinsons' marriage, had been for many years on a standing of intimacy with the family, and he and his wife had been annual visitors in their home. Since they were a childless couple, they became much attached to the young people as well as to their father, and Lavinia had often visited them in Salem.

Though his dignity carried great weight on the bench, Judge Lord's nature was warm and genial, and it was evident that a special sympathy was early established between him and Emily. She wrote of him after his death, "Calvary and May wrestled in his Nature," and her intuition was well fitted to bring the two into accord as she encountered them. Her mind, accustomed to cutting across all the conventional lines of thought in which his profession involved him, must have been both refreshing and stimulating to him. On her side, one can imagine, his keen and informed intelligence, lighted by the "May" in his nature, drew her out and enhanced the iridescent play of her own thoughts. She probably counted him as a correspondent even before her father's death, and afterward both she and Lavinia seem to have written to him with some regularity. None of the letters he received from them have been found, but a letter from him to Lavinia still exists that shows his attitude toward both sisters. It is undated, but can be quite accurately placed in March 1877 by the references in contains. Some excerpts follow:

There has not been a day since the receipt of your letter written in January, (I am ashamed to say) that I have not had it in my mind to write to you; but I have been either in court all [day] or in consultation with my associates or writing opinions and in the evening I have felt jaded with aching eyes and the listlessness and ennui of solitaire with one or more packs of cards has been the summit of my capacity; and I still have thought of you & of Emily, whose last note gave me a good deal of uneasiness, for knowing how entirely unselfish she is, and how unwilling to disclose any ailment, I fear that she has been more ill, than she has told me. I hope you will tell me particularly about her. . . .

I have felt anxious also about your health, for I know how wearing your incessant cares and the necessary anxieties of your situation are, but I hope that you will be able before a great while to run away from them and come and see us. Have you any idea how long it is since you have been here . . . .

Elizabeth [Mrs. Lord] has had a great deal of rheumatism or neuralgia or of both and a great part of the time is quite lame; but she is as uncomplaining and as thoughtful of everybody's comfort except her own as she has ever been, and is the only "crown of glory" I have ever, thus far, had. . . . Elizabeth joins me in love to you, and to all. I wish you would give me *full* accounts of the health of *each* of you. We often think and often talk of you if we do not to you. . . . With *much* love and *some* hope of amendment on my part, I remain

Affectionately

L.

Before the end of the year in which this letter was written, Judge Lord lost his "crown of glory." In his loneliness after the death of his wife, he seems to have been drawn more and more to the family at Amherst, and his special tenderness toward Emily deepened into another kind of love, which may have long been latent in his feeling for her. It was probably less than a year after the death of his wife that Emily began a series of letters to him that remained as drafts and copies among her own papers when she died. There is no way of knowing how closely they parallel the actual letters she sent him, and nothing else remains that could throw light on the relation that brought them into being. It is only as they reveal her own feeling that we can in some measure reconstruct the story of one of the most important emotional experiences of her life.

It is with a sense of diffidence, almost with apology, that one approaches these intimate expressions of love from a sensitive woman of forty-eight, for whom privacy was a paramount requirement, written to a man of dignity and authority eighteen years her senior and newly widowed. Neither the romantic sentiment of her own time nor the baldly realistic approach of a later generation allows for uncharted adventures of love under such circumstances. But love appears in many guises, and that it was a deep mutual attachment cannot be doubted. Emily Dickinson, who lived apart from the outer world's judgments and close to the essentials of the inner world, gave place only to the values that she could recognize as true for her, allowing life to happen as it would. The insistence of nature on trying to bring to completion and fruition each of its creatures is seen in human life in the tendency of man to find, at some time and in some way, an outlet for his various inherent forces. The time was ripe for Emily to find a kind of love she had not known before. Her earlier experience of love had been a part of her own inner upheaval, and whatever the degree of mutual attraction may have been, a relation on the plane of reality had hardly existed. Her years of solitary exploration of the deeper places of the soul and her ability to transform into art what she found there had brought her at last more fully into the stream of life itself. Her response to the loneliness of a man who had lost a loved partner of many years may have brought into flowering in him a renewal of an earlier passion, transforming the deep affection he felt for her, both as his friend's daughter and as a rare person in her own right, into the full love of a man for a woman. It is possible that he asked her to marry him, for the earlier letters show that an intimate relation had been discussed between them, and in a later letter she wrote:

> You said with loved timidity in asking me to your dear Home, you would "try not to make it unpleasant." So delicate a diffidence, how beautiful to see! I do not think a Girl extant has so divine a modesty.
> You even call me to your Breast with apology! Of what must my poor Heart be made?

From the first of the existing letters to those she wrote after four years of accepted love, freely expressed, it is clear that complete intimacy, either in marriage or without, was to be denied, yet the possibility of it was fully acknowledged between them. Even if the care of her invalid mother had not stood in the way of marriage, she probably would have found such a change impossible after so many years of personal independence. She knew that the best she had to give was of the spirit, and, although she felt her attitude called for forgiveness on the part of her lover, she was certain that it was right to keep their relations within the area where she could move most freely.

The fulfillment that came to Emily Dickinson through this attachment cannot be explained on a basis of the patterns established by average experience. The friendship of these two was outside the conventions, and was understood by themselves alone, though its significance was accepted by her brother and sister. The Judge's niece, who was deeply suspicious and resentful of what she did not understand, was not entirely unjustified in declaring that Emily was immoral, for Emily was not guided by the tenets of accepted behavior. Her morality was based on the laws of the spirit.

Emily's letters to Otis Lord, often playful, sometimes extravagant, suggest a background of dedication close to that of marriage. Yet after four years of correspondence with him on such a level, it was another man of whom she wrote as her "closest earthly friend" at the time of Dr. Wadsworth's death. To Judge Lord, whom she called in the earliest letter to him "My lovely Salem," she referred to Dr. Wadsworth as "my Philadelphia." No one could touch her on all sides, but her love could flow out to more than one man, each filling his own place in her life. Samuel Bowles had died before the intense period in her friendship with Otis Lord began, but her relation with him, too, had been important and unique. She found in him an enchantment of the spirit, a delight that was close to aesthetic emotion. On the other hand, her love for Lord was brought down to earth by mutual acceptance, and allowed to live on terms of personal attachment. Coming to her as he did in a period of transition, when she was still haunted by the memory of her father, and at first appearing in a fatherly aspect himself, he was able to bring her through to a new phase of experience by a love that was real, warm, and admittedly of an erotic nature. Her emotional life now found a center outside herself on which she could focus all her womanly feeling. It was her refuge from the sameness of the daily round and the source of strength and warmth in her relations with others. When she heard of Higginson's engagement to his second wife she wrote, "Till it has loved – no man or woman can become itself." She was just then finding this sort of self-realization in her own life.

There was now a time of expansion, reaching its height in 1880 and 1881, when the letters show a busy life filled with work and daily cares, in which she was supported by her weekly letters from her lover while she reached out with hand and heart to family and friends. There is a gaiety in some of the letters of this period that is hardly matched in any others. Not only little Gilbert, but her older nephew Ned became a playfellow with whom she shared ideas that amused her, and some of her most brilliant shafts of humor run through other letters of these years. At the same time her sympathy to friends to whom sorrow had come never flowed more warmly or simply, and her letters to them must have carried healing in their wealth of human understanding.

The comfort and joy of emotional fulfillment were not to last many years. The high tide of life had come late in the day and the inevitable ebb began as night advanced. She felt the first pull of the retreating waters when, on the first of April 1882, the Reverend Charles Wadsworth died. In the feeling of insecurity that followed this loss, she wrote to Judge Lord on the thirtieth of the month:

I am told it is only a pair of Sundays since you went from me. I feel it many years. Today is April's last – it has been an April of meaning to me. I have been in your Bosom. My Philadelphia has passed from Earth, and the Ralph Waldo Emerson – whose name my Father's Law Student taught me, has touched the secret Spring. Which Earth are we in?

Heaven, a Sunday or two ago – but that also has ceased –

Momentousness is ripening. I hope that all is firm. Could we yield each other to the impregnable chances till we had met once more?

Before the letter was mailed, "momentousness" had overtaken Judge Lord himself, for he was suddenly stricken with a serious illness from which he never fully recovered, and which marked the beginning of two years of declining powers. Six months later, when the mother whose little needs Emily had tended so long passed beyond her care, her death left Emily with more than a disengagement of the hands. It meant the loss of a tenderly cherished burden, such as a mother feels at the death of a hopelessly handicapped child whose going breaks the strongest tie to the reality of daily life. She wrote to Judge Lord:

I cannot conjecture a form of space without her timid face. Speaking to you as I feel, Dear, without that Dress of Spirit must be worn for most, Courage is quite changed.

Before another year had passed her courage was almost broken when the beloved child next door, eight-year-old Gilbert, was swept away in a violent illness of only a few days' duration. With his dearly loved person went far more of life than a child's experience could possibly encompass. To Emily his going meant not only the closing of a door to the bright region of childhood, where special values exist that are separate from those of the adult world, but the cutting off of the future with which he was her principal link. While she was still struggling to take up life again after the illness that followed this overwhelming blow, Judge Lord reached the end of his downward road and died, after a brief illness, in March 1884. Although the shock she felt at the time he was first stricken nearly two years before had probably been the greater, the event of his peaceful dying marked the culmination of her grief, made more poignant, doubtless, because its depth could not be disclosed to her friends. Life for her was now stripped of its creative relationships, and, while she still had the warmth of family affection in her devoted sister and brother, and friends with whom she felt the ties of common experience, death had undermined the structure in which she lived.

In the letters that were written in the intervals between ensuing periods of illness, the themes of loss and the memory of those that are gone lie heavily below the immediate concerns that occasioned the writing of them.

To attempt to speak of what has been, would be impossible. Abyss has no Biographer –

. . . every jostling of the Spirit barbs the Loss afresh – even the coming out of the Sun after an Hour's Rain, intensifies their Absence –

Show me Eternity, and I will show you Memory –
Both in one package lain
And lifted back again –

In one letter to an old friend whom she had not seen for many years, she said simply, "The Dyings have been too deep for me." Death, which in earlier times had plagued and followed her as a fascinating riddle, a distant terror, or a grim lover, was now a heavy encroaching shadow, immediate and inevitable, as great a mystery as ever, but unanswerable and all demanding.

Always reticent in personal matters, Emily did not write

to her friends about the inner adjustments that must have come with failing health, and the record of her thoughts during the closing years is found oftener between the lines than in them. When the ill body made the spirit dim, she was, in her own words to Higginson, "bereft of Book and Thought." When she was able to take up her pencil again, her innate courtesy and consideration demanded that she write little notes of thanks to inquiring neighbors, or letters to friends that dwelt more on their concerns than her own. Among her papers, after her death, were many scraps and fragments of drafts of poems and letters, some of which may have been written during that time, but the handwriting of such notes and jottings shows less variation from year to year than that of letters actually sent, and consequently they have not been definitely dated. Such a fragment as the following could very well have been the substance of a poem projected in her later years but never written:

The consciousness of subsiding power is too startling to be admitted by men – but [best] comprehended by the meadow over which the Flood has quivered (comprehended perhaps by the Meadow, over which Floods have [quivered] – rumbled –), when the waters return to their kindred, and the tillage (acre –) is left alone –

Two poems that can with some certainty be dated about 1884 betray the despairing moments she passed through during that difficult year.

> Oh Future! thou secreted peace
> Or subterranean wo –
> Is there no wandering route of grace
> That leads away from thee –

TO LIVE IS ENDOWMENT

No circuit sage of all the course
Descried by cunning Men
To balk thee of thy sacred Prey –
Advancing to thy Den –

In this poem she is still in the midst of a struggle, but in the
second she has capitulated and gives herself up, while still
alive, to the experience of death she can now share with those
who are gone.

So give me back to Death –
The Death I never feared
Except that it deprived of thee –
And now, by Life deprived,
In my own Grave I breathe
And estimate it's size –
It's size is all that Hell can guess –
And all that Heaven was –

The dissolving world in which Emily now found herself
brought her within two years into a position that is seldom
reached at her age by those who live in the ever shifting
circles of a broader environment. It is probable that a lifelong
physical weakness began at this time to develop into the
disease that brought about her death two years later, but in
the finer adjustments of mind and body it is impossible to tell
which is cause and which is effect. Death was now the
medium through which she saw life. With the pervasion of
a sense of finality there seems to have come no clear and
steady vision of immortality such as sometimes illumines the
last years of the aged. When at the time of Judge Lord's
dangerous illness she had written to Washington Gladden,
whose liberal preaching and writing had brought him into

prominence, to ask if immortality were true, she was seeking help for herself, though she made her friend's peace of mind her excuse. After his death she made it clear in a letter to his friend Benjamin Kimball that he had found peace of mind in a different way.

Perhaps to solidify his faith was for him impossible, and if for him, how more, for us! . . .
Neither fearing Extinction, nor prizing Redemption, he believed alone. Victory was his Rendezvous –

While Dr. Wadsworth lived she leaned on the security of his faith when her own wavered, as she implied when she wrote to Charles Clark in October 1883:

These thoughts disquiet me, and the great friend is gone, who could solace them. Do they disturb you?

> The Spirit lasts – but in what mode –
> Below, the Body speaks,
> But as the Spirit furnishes –
> Apart, it never talks –
> The Music in the Violin
> Does not emerge alone
> But Arm in Arm with Touch, yet Touch
> Alone – is not a Tune –
> The Spirit lurks within the Flesh
> Like Tides within the Sea
> That make the Water live, estranged
> What would the Either be?
> Does that know – now – or does it cease –
> That which to this is done,
> Resuming at a mutual date
> With every future one?
> Instinct pursues the Adamant,
> Exacting this Reply –

TO LIVE IS ENDOWMENT

Adversity if it may be, or
Wild Prosperity,
The Rumor's Gate was shut so tight
Before my Mind was sown,
Not even a Prognostic's Push
Could make a Dent thereon –

The final quatrain, so forceful in its denial of the slightest possibility of finding an answer to her questions that she used it in slightly variant form in three separate poems, betrays the urgency of her search. She seemed to assume that for Dr. Wadsworth himself the Heaven he believed in was realized at his death, but closer to her own mind was Judge Lord's open uncertainty. The glimpses of immortality she had been given all through her life in moments of ecstatic insight from an unknown source had never become for her a solid foundation for faith in conscious life after death. One of the last datable poems, left unfinished, as if the thought itself were never completed, is in a mood of protest against the inescapable, omnipresent concept of immortality.

Why should we hurry – why indeed
When every way we fly
We are molested equally
by immortality
no respite from the inference
that this which is begun
though where it's labors lie
A bland uncertainty
Besets the sight
This mighty night

The disjointedness of the last four lines, obviously jotted down for later testing, and the force of the word "Tragedy," underlined twice, standing in the center of the page, portray a mood in which the prospect of absolute extinction would be preferable to the torment of the unknowable.

It need not be assumed, however, that Emily lived in an atmosphere of gloom. On the contrary, when the ties that held her to life were cut one by one, she seemed to find new freedom and detachment that brought added meaning to the smallest events. She followed the happenings in the lives of friends and neighbors with as much concern as she had felt in earlier years, and in her letters to them was able to share their feelings and meet their moods, writing to each in the vein best suited to his age or type of mind. She never lost her joy in playing with words, and her sense of fun still lurked ready for provocation, even under grim circumstances. After a burglary had occurred at Austin's house in November 1885, the month that marked the beginning of her last long period of illness, she wrote to Ned, "Burglaries have become so frequent, is it quite safe to leave the Golden Rule out over night?" It was scarcely a month before she died that she gave her aunt Mrs. Currier an account of a local scandal, commenting, "Dont you think Fumigation ceased when Father died?"

There was even an intensification of perception in her last years, which she recognized when she wrote to Mrs. Holland late in 1884:

All grows strangely emphatic, and I think if I should see you again, I sh'd begin every sentence with "I say unto you –" The Bible dealt with the Centre, not with the Circumference –

Everything was seen in the intensely clear light that sometimes occurs just after sundown. It is even possible that she came nearer than ever before to arresting the transitory ecstasy of which all her life she had received fleeting experiences. One of the last poems she completed gives ecstasy a place of supreme value in a world from which everything else had been taken away. It seems to have had great meaning for her at the time, for she incorporated it into letters to three friends during the year 1885, in which it appears as verse in letters to Mr. and Mrs. Loomis and to Helen Hunt Jackson, and as prose in a little note to Samuel Bowles the younger, each time given a different connotation.

> Take all away from me, but leave me Ecstasy,
> And I am richer then than all my Fellow Men –
> Ill it becometh me to dwell so wealthily
> When at my very Door are those possessing more,
> In abject poverty –

Her business was no longer Circumference, but, as she said of the Bible, the Centre. Of immortality as a future state she was never sure, and human love was too vulnerable to loss to be relied on as a force with which to encounter death. Ecstasy, the gift of the gods, was the living flame at the center of the poet's own being. After all else was taken away she found the spark still burning. It was as a poet that she must take leave of life, sure of nothing except the unnamed meaning at the core of life itself.

PART TWO

MY FRIENDS ARE MY "ESTATE"

Among the infinite variety of human beings, any combination of two creates a new situation. Except in the most superficial relations, no one shows exactly the same aspects of himself to different people. Those whom Emily Dickinson chose as life-long friends had each a special meaning for her, and each responded to her qualities according to his own nature. Through sensitive adjustment, her letters reflect the unique character of each relation and tell as much of the personality of the recipient as of the writer. The three friendships discussed here reveal separate facets of her mind and take widely varying places in her life.

JOSIAH GILBERT HOLLAND
AND
ELIZABETH CHAPIN HOLLAND

"You were so long so faithful"

When Emily Dickinson was twenty-two and in need of a broader social base than she found in her family and among the former schoolmates whom she was fast outgrowing, she formed a new friendship into which she threw herself joyfully. The affection that grew up on both sides developed into a firm and comforting friendship lasting to the end of her life.

On August 15, 1851, Josiah Gilbert Holland received an honorary degree of A.M. from Amherst College. On this occasion he was almost certainly invited to the house of Edward Dickinson, who, as treasurer of the college and a leading citizen, took an active interest in such events. Dr. Holland was already known to the Dickinson family through his writing in the *Springfield Republican,* of which they were constant readers. It is possible, too, that the families had been acquainted in preceding generations, for Emily Dickinson's forebears and those of Mrs. Holland had lived in the Connecticut Valley from the earliest years of the settlement. Although Dr. Holland's family had not established itself in the region until later, he himself was born in Belchertown, only a few miles east of Amherst, and spent much of his youth in Northampton, seven miles to the west.

During the nineteenth century, the Connecticut Valley towns had an integrated life of their own. In pioneer days a hundred miles of uninhabited forest had lain between the valley and its parent colony on Massachusetts Bay, and even in Emily Dickinson's time something of this separateness lingered, though the people of the region were by then in easy contact with the outside world, turning quite as readily to New York as to Boston for their cultural associations. Their way of living still had a rural quality, but a satisfying social life had grown up on the solid foundation that had been laid by the earlier generations. Solomon Bulkley Griffin, writing of Springfield in the first half of the nineteenth century, said, "Larger recognition was given to the cultivated side of life, and those who paid heed to the amenities were highly regarded. So came a recognized aristocracy of education, brains and accomplishment."

If the Dickinsons first met Dr. Holland at the Amherst commencement of 1851, it would have been without his wife, for the Hollands' eldest daughter was born shortly after that date. In the following years, he visited Amherst a number of times in connection with his work on the *Springfield Republican,* and seems to have become acquainted with the whole Dickinson family before Mrs. Holland had an opportunity to meet them. When, in the spring of 1853 Amherst celebrated its connection with the larger towns by the open-

ing of the Amherst and Belchertown Railway, an excursion
took place that brought three hundred people on a special
train from New London. Emily Dickinson wrote an account
of the events to her brother Austin, who was then studying
law at Harvard. After describing the celebration, for which
their father was chief marshal, she continued, "Dr Holland
was here and called to see us — seemed very pleasant indeed,
inquired for you, and asked mother if Vinnie and I might
come and see them in Springfield."

Mr. and Mrs. Dickinson may have hesitated to accept the
invitation for their daughters before they became acquainted
with the hostess, and they probably urged Dr. Holland to
bring his wife to see them when he came again to Amherst.
It was not long before he did so, for Emily wrote to her
brother on the tenth of July:

Dr Holland and his wife, spent last Friday with us — came unexpectedly — we had a charming time, and have promised to visit them after
Commencement. They asked all about you, and Dr Holland's wife
expressed a great desire to see you — He said you would be a Judge —
there was no help for it — you must certainly be a Judge! We had
Champagne for dinner, and a very fine time — We were so sorry you
were not here, and Dr and Mrs Holland expressed their regret many
times —

Emily alluded to this first meeting several years later, when
she wrote to Mrs. Holland an account of how the family
moved back to the family mansion. "We cannot talk and
laugh more, in the parlor where we met," she said, "but we
learned to love for aye, there, so it is just as well." The gala
atmosphere of the occasion made an auspicious opening for

the development of the friendship. With parental approval now assured, the girls accepted the invitation that had been given earlier, and visited the Hollands in Springfield in September.

At the time of this first visit, Dr. Holland had passed his thirty-fourth birthday, and his wife was thirty. Emily was enough younger to find exhilaration in the society of this couple whose experience of life exceeded hers, and whose relation to each other must have looked like the ideal one for which every girl hopes. In their close mutual dependence throughout their married life, the Hollands kept the brightness of their admiration for each other undimmed. They were opposite in temperament and their physical characteristics were strongly contrasting. Elizabeth Chapin Holland was small in body but forceful in spirit. She was vivacious and brisk, though always gracious in manner. Part of her charm lay in her directness and candor, and she was endowed with the sure feeling for reality often known as common sense. In contrast to her short stature and fair coloring, her husband's tall, erect figure, black eyes, and straight black hair gave him what one of his friends described as the appearance of an Indian chief. Together with his natural dignity, he had a simple and warmly responsive manner, the expression of a genuine interest in people.

Josiah Holland — whom his family called by his middle name, Gilbert — had grown up in poverty as a member of a large family of good inheritance but little practical sense. His father, Harrison Holland, wandered from town to town in search of better opportunities, taking with him little but a

Puritanical piety, an inventive mind, and a childlike faith in the future. The public benefited far more than he did from Harrison Holland's inventions, for he never obtained a patent, and his ideas were taken up by others who were able to use them to better advantage. Dr. Holland's biographer, Mrs. Plunkett, tells us that as late as 1894, when her book was written, raw silk from China still came wound on reels made from his design.

When the family reached Northampton, Josiah took matters into his own hands, found a job as a chore boy in the house of a prominent citizen, went to high school, and began to prepare himself to fulfill the destiny which Mrs. Plunkett tells us he had always known was his — to be "an educated gentleman." That this boyish ambition was by no means a matter of externals is shown in the reminiscences of a friend of his early years which appeared in the *Springfield Republican* at the time of his death. The two boys had often spent nights together at each other's house, and his friend recalled one cold winter morning when Josiah stood half-dressed in the unheated bedroom, his face radiant with enthusiasm, a shoe in one hand and a copy of Thomson's *Seasons* in the other, reading aloud passages from the poem with a running commentary of appreciative analysis.

Josiah wanted to be a professional man. His upbringing would have inclined him toward the church, but he could not afford the years of study that were needed to prepare him for the ministry. He was not attracted to the law, but the medical profession appealed to him because of its direct relation to people's needs. Since only two years' training was required at that time, he decided to become a physician. Following customary procedure, he studied in the office of two prominent doctors in Northampton; and to qualify for the medical degree, he completed his course with two short terms of lectures at the Berkshire Medical College at Pittsfield.

The title "Doctor" clung to Josiah Holland all his life, though he soon dropped the practice of medicine. The most noteworthy fact that is remembered about him as a physician is his strong belief in fresh air at a time when the sick were closeted with their diseases and protected from the light of day. He had lost three sisters, two by tuberculosis, and he was so thoroughly convinced that a life in the open air would have saved them that when he married he took his young wife with him in his buggy wherever he went, to build up her health. But, as a doctor he was a failure, chiefly because he was more interested in writing verses than in dosing his patients. Struggling against the cramping effects of poverty, he had early sought enlightenment and satisfaction for his aesthetic longings in the few books that were available to him, and his desire to expand his spirit through things of beauty became a part of the pattern of his life. In his efforts to educate himself he had learned to think independently, and his active mind not only craved an outlet but required a moral purpose for its expression.

As a minister he would have given his message to a limited group. As it was, each step he took pushed him a little farther toward the position he was to achieve as lay preacher to a nationwide audience. He started a weekly paper which failed after a few months; then, feeling that a married man should earn an assured income, he turned to teaching. In 1847 he took a position in a business college at Richmond, Virginia, and the following year went to Vicksburg, Mississippi, as superintendent of schools. From Vicksburg, in January 1848, he sent a lively account of the seventeen-day journey from Springfield and addressed it to Samuel Bowles, the young editor of *The Springfield Daily Republican*, who printed it in three installments in an important column of the paper.

When the fatal illness of Mrs. Holland's mother brought them back to Springfield in the spring of 1849, Dr. Holland found an opening in the field of work most congenial to him. While still at Vicksburg he had sent the *Springfield Republican* a series of articles entitled "Sketches of Plantation Life," which probably led to his being asked to fill the post made vacant by the death of the associate editor. The articles appeared anonymously as "Three Weeks on a Cotton Plantation" some months later. Many years afterward Dr. Holland told the story of his arrival in Springfield — how, on driving down the street from the station, he saw Samuel Bowles standing at the entrance to the *Republican* office, and how the same thought flashed through the minds of both. Action followed at once, and when Mr. Bowles asked him to fill the vacant position, the young man who had tried to be a doctor and a schoolteacher, but who never could keep from writing, accepted the offer instantly.

The daily *Republican* was then five years old. In 1844, when Samuel Bowles, Jr. persuaded his father to turn his weekly paper into a daily, he made some innovations which developed this small-town sheet into a paper of national repute. Political news and comment and a pronounced stand on matters of national importance superseded the items of local interest, bits of general information, timetables, and advertisements of patent medicines that had formed the principal part of the earlier paper. Now, by asking Dr. Holland to join him, Mr. Bowles brought in an element that broadened the scope of the paper still more and added to its popularity not only in western Massachusetts, but in other parts of the country as well. As associate editor, Dr. Holland entered into the task of opening up for the common man opportunities to broaden his mind and enrich his soul. He added more extensive book reviews and other cultural articles to the paper, together with editorial essays on manners and morals in public and personal life.

The conduct of life was supremely important to New Englanders, who looked chiefly to their ministers for leadership in moral and social questions. But the beginnings of modern scientific thought were bringing changes into their lives which made the guidance of the local pulpits seem inadequate. The little sermons that now came to them as editorials in this daily paper were written from a fresh point of view by a young man who drew his ideas directly from his own observations and experience of life. There was a robust quality in his writing which was free from the sanctimonious platitudes of the pulpit. Under the humorous comment that often gave a trivial surface to the matter, one felt the convictions of this man who loved God with the same fervor with which his ancestors had feared Him. Within the bounds imposed by his unyielding principles, his spirit flowered freely and innocently.

The happy atmosphere that Emily Dickinson found in the Hollands' home was due quite as much to the character of the wife as of the husband. Everything Elizabeth Holland did was marked by a quality which Emily thought of as bird-like. This came as much from the quickness of her mind as from the nimbleness of her small body. A characteristic that must have endeared her especially to Emily was her ability to lift the drab or the ponderous into a lighter atmosphere. She had the gift of meeting people on their own ground, yet retaining her own individuality. She could be crisply out-spoken, but never bitter, and her quick humor saved many an awkward situation.

Born Elizabeth Chapin, Mrs. Holland had been accus-tomed to self-reliance since childhood. A descendant of Samuel Chapin, one of the pioneer leaders of the Springfield community, she had been left without resources by the early death of her father. At ten she was taken into the family of an uncle in Albany, where she was given a good education at the Albany Female Academy, a school of high standing at that time. In Albany, Elizabeth found a different social en-vironment from the one in which she had spent her child-hood. The aristocratic system of the early Dutch settlers formed the background of society in the New York state capital, and the descendants of the patroons still owned vast estates in the surrounding country. Social classes remained distinct, and the family with whom Elizabeth lived joined in the gaieties of the holidays which were celebrated according to Dutch custom, and, as members of the upper class, dis-pensed charity to the poor. Elizabeth formed close ties with the members of this household, but remained with them only through her school years. As the eldest daughter, she was needed at home as soon as her education was completed, and so, while still under twenty, she returned to the less sophisticated life of Springfield.

When Elizabeth Chapin married, she shared her home as a matter of course with her husband's widowed mother and her own younger sister. She was a good and thrifty housekeeper, and during the earlier years of her marriage she not only patched and darned, but made her own clothes and some of her husband's. Although she was completely fulfilled in the activities that centered in her home, her husband relied upon her as his best adviser on all important decisions.

At the Hollands' no one was afraid to laugh, and if the theater was still beyond the pale along with prize fights and horse racing, it did not matter much, because the theater hardly presented a problem to the inhabitants of western Massachusetts, and there were plenty of things at home to laugh about. The three children found companionship with their parents as natural as their unrestricted play. In spite of the fullness of Mrs. Holland's days, she always had time for her friends, and her parlor was a center where new books were shared and discussed and music was a part of the daily life. Although her husband's fine tenor voice was used only to the glory of God on Sunday, on weekdays he sang the old ballads with equal enthusiasm. In the early years of their friendship, a visit to the Hollands brought to Emily Dickinson a special release of spirit that infused her days with a glow for a long time afterward. Her earliest letters to them, full of the expansiveness of a new and youthful affection, contain such passages as this:

> I love to write to you — it gives my heart a holiday and sets the bells to ringing. If prayers had any answers to them, you were all here to-night, but I seek and I don't find, and knock and it is not opened. Wonder if God is just — presume he is, however, and t'was only a blunder of Matthew's.
>
> I think mine is the case, where when they ask an egg, they get a scorpion, for I keep wishing for you, keep shutting up my eyes and looking toward the sky, asking with all my might for you, and yet you do not come. I wrote to you last week, but thought you would laugh at me, and call me sentimental, so I kept my lofty letter for "Adolphus Hawkins, Esq."

The excitement Emily felt in the companionship of these new friends was tinged with the luster of her own love of life. It was their qualities of heart, their spontaneity and natural-ness, rather than any intellectual stimulus received from them, that formed the basis of their friendship. The dam of her pent-up emotions overflowed, and the affection she poured out with such abundance might have become a burden. That the friendship with Mrs. Holland was sustained through more than thirty years may have been due in good part to the older woman's balanced nature, which enabled her to guide the flood of Emily's affection into channels of loyalty and understanding.

At first Emily seems to have fallen in love with the Holland family as a unit, but later it was with Mrs. Holland that her intimacy grew. Although she sometimes wrote to Dr. Hol-land separately, he never played for her a special role as literary adviser or spiritual guide. When she wrote in an early letter, "*The Republican* seems to us like a letter from you, and we break the seal and read it eagerly," she was including Vinnie in her statement and referring to the Hollands collectively. When she began to send poems to her friends, she included the Hollands among those to whom she sent them, but there is no suggestion in any of her letters that she would like a criticism from the literary editor of the *Springfield Republican*. Neither did she express any opinion of his writing except in a single phrase in a letter of January 1856, before her own serious work had begun, when she sent her thanks to him for his "exquisite hymn." The poem he had sent was probably his Christmas carol "There's a star in the sky." Since none of her letters from the Hollands have been preserved, there is no way of knowing what comments they may have made on the poems received from her. The remark attributed to Dr. Holland, that they were "too etherial for publication," is the only intimation of his estimate of her genius. She was doubtless aware that she belonged in a different literary atmosphere from the one in which he was at home, and it was as a person rather than a writer that she cherished him.

The *Springfield Republican* did not long absorb Holland's energies, for his interests demanded wider scope than journalism could offer. His first book, a *History of Western Massachusetts*, was published serially in the paper. This was followed in 1857 by a novel, *The Bay Path*, a story of the early settlers in Springfield, and the next year by *Bitter-Sweet*, a long narrative poem of New England life which gained such popularity that it is said to have sold in larger numbers than any other American poem except *Hiawatha*. In his review of it in the *Atlantic Monthly*, Lowell said:

It is not free from faults of taste nor a certain commonplaceness of metre, but Mr. Holland always saves himself in some expression so simply poetical, some image so fresh and natural, the harvest of his own heart and eye, that we are ready to forgive him all his faults in our thankfulness at finding the soul of Theocritus transmigrated into the body of a Yankee. . . We mean it as very high praise when we say that *Bitter-Sweet* is one of the few books that have found the secret of drawing up and assimilating the juices of this New World of ours.

The poems and novels that followed were widely read and as enthusiastically received by the general public as they were neglected or pulled apart by the critics. Realistic rather than romantic in conception, his stories, both in prose and verse, formed for many of his readers a link between literature and life, and introduced to them views that were just enough broader than theirs to lead them on to better reading. A special correspondent, writing to the *Chicago Tribune*, on October 20, 1881, shortly after his death, said:

Less than half a century ago there was not considered sufficient material for a tolerable work of fiction in this country, and J. G. Holland was prominent in producing an interest in themes and subjects drawn entirely from American scenes and events.

By 1865, Dr. Holland had become a highly successful author and popular lecturer, receiving not only applause but abundant material rewards as well. His was the kind of success story that Americans have always loved, and the fact that the subject of it was a moralist made it especially attractive to many of his own generation. In part, it is the story of a man who happened to be on hand to meet a need which he was peculiarly fitted to fill, but it is also a story of an inner drive, frugal habits, and hard work, in all of which his wife's share was equal to his own.

Emily Dickinson never called Mrs. Holland by her first name, but in 1859 she began to use the title "Sister" and remained faithful to it throughout the rest of her life. Its adoption seems to have been the result of an appeal for help in a social dilemma at a time when Lavinia was away on a visit. Explaining how she had been detected in running away from important visitors, Emily said:

> Not alone to thank you for your sweet note, is my errand, dear Mrs. Holland, tho' I do indeed, but will you please to help me?
>
> I guess I have done wrong – I don't know certainly, but Austin tells me so, and he is older than I, and knows more of ordinances.
>
> When Vinnie is here – I ask her; if she says I sin, I say, "Father, I have sinned" – if she sanctions me, I am not afraid, but Vinnie is gone now, and to my sweet elder sister, in the younger's absence, something guides my feet.

Her next letter began: "Sister."

One would suppose that with the close relation implied by the new title, the letters of the next few years would have been frequent, but on the contrary, no letters remain from the period between 1860 and 1865. No single reason has been found to account for the gap, which covers both the period of the Civil War and of Emily's own inner revolution. Perhaps Mrs. Holland lost or destroyed some letters when the family moved in 1862 to the new house they had built on a wooded bluff outside the city, but such a loss would not account for the three years still remaining before the next of the existing letters was written. Another possibility is that Emily found her newer friends more important to her during those years. Her friendship with Mr. and Mrs. Bowles had begun shortly before, and her correspondence with Mr. Bowles was at its most intense point in the early 1860's. It was in 1862, also, that she started writing to Thomas Wentworth Higginson, marking her first acknowledgment that she was a poet.

It was natural that the correspondence should lapse during the two long periods of exile Emily spent in Cambridge in 1864 and 1865, when she was under the care of a Boston oculist. The use of her pen was forbidden while her eyes were under treatment, and she wrote only the most necessary letters, but, though expression was limited, her loyalties remained undiminished. When the thread of connection between the friends was renewed again in the autumn of 1865 after Emily had returned to Amherst, relations were still close and news was being exchanged, perhaps through other members of the family. The correspondence was resumed, and visits became frequent when the coming to Amherst in 1865 of Mrs. Holland's cousins, the Laurenus Clark Seelyes, brought her often to the town.

In May 1868, the Hollands found a tenant for their house, and, following the custom of the time for those who could afford to do so, the whole family sailed for Europe, where they spent the next two years. Emily's use of geographical names to evoke images had little to do with the realities met in travel, and the ocean seemed to her an insuperable barrier between her and her friends. When Samuel Bowles went to Europe in 1862, she wrote to him, "You sleep so far, how can I know you hear?" Whether it was because she did not try to reach Mrs. Holland while she was away, or because that practical lady kept her correspondence tidied up as she went, to the loss of later generations, the unfortunate fact is that no letters from those years have been preserved.

When the family came home in the spring of 1870, Dr. Holland turned all his energies into an enterprise he had planned while abroad — the launching of a new magazine, *Scribner's Monthly*. According to Robert Underwood Johnson, who was later a member of his staff, Dr. Holland and his business partner, Roswell Smith, aimed at nothing less than leadership in political, religious, artistic, and social opinion. Although this goal was somewhat too high for realization, the magazine was successful from the start. The Dickinsons were among the first subscribers, and Emily alluded in many of her letters to the stories and articles she had read in it. The new venture soon made it necessary for the Hollands to give up their home in Springfield, but the move to New York, in spite of the increased distance, seemed only to strengthen the friendship.

By far the most important part of Emily's correspondence with Mrs. Holland occurred after 1870, and the letters to this friend have a character that is distinct. Each phase of the spirit that she passed through is reflected in them, but the qualities of the person to whom she was writing helped to shape them. In the first years of their friendship, Emily had seen the Hollands as objects for admiration, whose affection she craved, but whose lives moved in an orbit that was separated from her own. When she did not hear from them she "concluded that one of the bright things had gone forever more." After life had deepened and made more positive her own identity, she was able to form a relation in which she carried an equal share. There is a sense of ease in the letters of the eighteen seventies and eighties — even when the language is inclined toward the sententious — that springs from the assurance of being accepted. She was writing to a proven friend from whom she need not hide. She welcomed every contact with Mrs. Holland and eagerly anticipated her visits long after she had closed her doors to her neighbors. At the "mansion" on Main Street the visitor was shared by the entire household, from Mrs. Dickinson, who found Mrs. Holland "so social" to Irish Maggie in the kitchen, who, in Emily's words, deemed her "a mistress most to be desired." The Hollands had always been fond of Lavinia, whose quick wit and exuberant interest in human affairs made her an entertaining companion. Mrs. Holland, with her practical sense and lightness of touch, bringing with her a taste of the larger world, yet belonging with an indissoluble tie to the New England scene, had some specific value for each of these disparate persons. To Emily, who alone called her "Sister," she continued to bring the release of spirit that had marked their first acquaintance.

On the other side, it is evident that Emily's letters were welcomed and cherished even when their forms of expression sounded so strange to the recipient's ears that she later described them in a letter to Mrs. Todd as "quaint." The subject matter is sometimes trivial, and the style aphoristic, but the emotional content with which Emily fills it is rich, because of the warmth of human relations implied in it. Such a letter as the following, written in 1871, is an example:

> I have a fear I did not thank you for the thoughtful Candy. Could you conscientiously dispel it by saying that I did? Generous little Sister!
> I will protect the Thimble till it reaches Home —
> Even the Thimble has it's Nest!
> The Parting I tried to smuggle resulted in quite a Mob at last! The Fence is the only Sanctuary. That no one invades because no one suspects it.
> Why the Thief ingredient accompanies all Sweetness Darwin does not tell us.
> Each expiring Secret leaves an Heir, distracting still.
> Our unfinished interview like the Cloth of Dreams, cheapens other fabrics.
> That Possession fairest lies that is least possest.
> Transport's mighty price is no more than he is worth —
> Would we sell him for it? That is all his Test.
> Dont affront the Eyes —
> Little Despots govern worst.
> Vinnie leaves me Monday — Spare me your remembrance while I buffet Life and Time without —
>
> Emily.

The framework of the letter consists only of the small happenings incident to an afternoon call, when Mrs. Holland brought Emily a box of candy and carried her sewing with her to work on while they talked. After she left, she discovered that her thimble was missing, and Emily was writing to tell her it had been found. Upon these trivialities Emily built a work of art, full of the thoughts that even the slightest event could precipitate. Within the structure thus made, the feeling tone of the letter lies wholly in the implications. She knew that her "little sister" would forgive her if her manners had failed because her pleasure in seeing her friend was greater than in the gift she had brought. She had hoped to see her alone before they parted, but her maneuvers had been unsuccessful. In spite of her disappointment, she had found the unfinished interview all the more precious because it was hindered. She was concerned about Mrs. Holland's suffering from a disease of the eyes that she had quietly endured for a number of years, and begged her to save them. Finally, she was sure of her friend's understanding when she confessed her dependence on Vinnie as her link with the outside world.

Emily followed the events in the lives of her friends with an attitude that went beyond sympathy. When the news reached her that it was necessary for Mrs. Holland to have an operation for the removal of one eye, she did not bemoan the loss, but expressed admiration for the way her friend faced the ordeal, closing her short letter with "Be secure of this, that whatever waver – her Gibraltar's Heart is firm." Every important event in the Holland family was noticed, whether it was such a misfortune as this or the happy enlargement of their life by the building of a summer home on the St. Lawrence River. Not only the engagements of their daughters, but even the twinges of rheumatism that sometimes plagued Mrs. Holland's shoulder brought tender responses from Emily. She knew that the Hollands would laugh with her when some ludicrous aspect of daily life set in motion her special form of fantasy. In the spring of 1881 she began a letter:

MY FRIENDS ARE MY "ESTATE"

Dear Sister.

We are making a few simple repairs, what Dickens would call qualifications and aspects – and looking in Vinnie's Basket for the Lightning Rod, which she had mislaid, "What *would* Mrs Holland think" said Vinnie?

"I would inquire," I said.

I can always rely on your little Laugh, which is what the Essayist calls "the immortal Peewee."

Emily could rely on more than Mrs. Holland's "little laugh," for it was she whom Emily chose to address and forward her letters to Dr. Wadsworth in Philadelphia. We find the first allusion to the practice in a short note written about 1876, with Mrs. Holland's name on the outside of the folded sheet to distinguish it from the enclosure. The note reads:

I once more come, with my little Load – Is it too heavy, Sister?

You remember from whom I quoted, when you brought me the Clover?

"I find your Benefits no Burden, Jane."

Had I only a Postal, with your Smile, I should sleep safer.

Emily.

Both the allusion to the clover and a more explicit statement of the nature of the little load were given in later letters. Although Mrs. Holland does not seem to have been present at the funeral of Edward Dickinson, she had later visited his grave, carrying back to Emily a spray of clover that was blooming there. Several months after her father's death, Emily ended a letter full of the loneliness of his absence,

Thank you for the Affection. It helps me up the Stairs at Night, where as I passed my Father's Door – I used to think was safety. The Hand that plucked the Clover – I seek, and am

Emily.

134

That she sought the same hand to forward her letters to Dr. Wadsworth is clearly stated in a letter written early in December 1877:

> I enclose a Note, which if you would lift as far as Philadelphia, if it did not tire your Arms – would please me so much.
> Would the Doctor be willing to address it? Ask him, with my love.

The Hollands knew that she preferred not to submit her private correspondence to the scrutiny of the village postmaster, and probably were aware that she asked other friends also to address some of her letters for her. Two neighbors in Amherst, both elderly men — Luke Sweetser and her father's cousin George Montague — served her in this capacity in the late 1870's and early 1880's, but that it was the Hollands to whom she had entrusted her letters to Dr. Wadsworth over a long stretch of time seems to be confirmed in a letter written in 1879:

> I ask you to ask your Doctor will he be so kind as to write the name of my Philadelphia friend on the Note within, and your little Hand will take it to him –
> You were so long so faithful, Earth would not seem homelike without your little sunny Acts –

The use of the word "were" instead of the continuing "have been," which one would expect to find in this connection, suggests that the little acts of kindness had been performed more often in the past. This is, in fact, the last time that such a request appears in the letters, though Dr. Wadsworth's death did not occur until nearly three years later. It could not have been from any lack of willingness on the part of the Hollands that Emily no longer asked this slight favor. It may, on the other hand, have been her recognition of Dr. Holland's failing health, which began to cause the family anxiety at about that time, since her request involved his assistance. Emily's desire for their protection could never have seemed unreasonable to the Hollands. They accepted her differences, and were glad to help her to fulfill her living after her own pattern. She probably never confided in them some phases of her life that touched her most closely, for each friend had a distinct place. She makes this clear in the same letter from which the extract above was taken — a letter written with special freedom and overtones of gaiety. "Should you ask what had happened here," she said, "I should say nothing perceptible. Sweet latent events – too shy to confide." Since her relation with Judge Lord was at this time reaching its most vital period, she may have been sharing some of its warmth without betraying the source from which it came.

After the first symptoms of heart trouble in 1878 had given Dr. Holland warning that he must cut down his activities, he began to reorganize the affairs of *Scribner's Monthly*. He remained so well, however, through the next three years, that when death came to him suddenly in October 1881 it was wholly unexpected. He had been actively engaged in bringing about the changes that occurred when the magazine, hitherto published under the Scribner name, was taken over by the newly organized Century Company, and issued under the name *The Century*. The telegram announcing his death to the Dickinsons brought an immediate reply from Emily, followed by several notes in quick succession as she tenderly followed in sympathy the first grief-stricken days of her friend.

Without regard to her own questioning of the accepted views on life after death, she recognized the beliefs of her friends as valid for them. One letter in this series especially shows her attitude toward the Hollands, whose religious beliefs and intellectual outlook were never fully her own, but whose personal qualities bound her to them with enduring affection.

> After a while, dear, you will remember that there is a heaven — but you can't now. Jesus will excuse it. He will remember his shorn lamb.
>
> The lost one was on such childlike terms with the Father in Heaven. He has passed from confiding to comprehending — perhaps but a step.
>
> The *safety* of a beloved lost is the first anguish. With you, that is peace.
>
> I shall never forget the Doctor's prayer, my first morning with you — so simple, so believing. *That* God must be a friend — *that* was a different God — and I almost felt warmer myself, in the midst of a tie so sunshiny.
>
> I am yearning to know if he knew he was fleeing — if he spoke to you. Dare I ask if he suffered? Some one will tell me a very little, when they have the strength . . . Cling tight to the hearts that will not let you fall.
>
> Emily.

In the years that followed Emily saw less of her friends, but after Dr. Holland died, and when her own losses grew year by year, the letters she wrote to Mrs. Holland showed a greater simplicity and a depth of heart that gave them special richness. Nothing was too small to engage her interest, and she never lost her pleasure in calling out Mrs. Holland's "little laugh." It was as if the larger issues of life had been resolved, and an understanding of them could be assumed on both sides. Yet, in the crisis of her illness after the death of her little nephew Gilbert, in October 1883, she felt free to express her own anguish to such a faithful friend.

"Open the Door, open the Door, they are waiting for me," was Gilbert's sweet command in delirium. *Who* were waiting for him, all we possess we would give to know – Anguish at last opened it, and he ran to the little Grave at his Grandparents' feet – All this and more, though *is* there more? More than Love and Death? Then tell me it's name!

Always fearful of losing her friends, Emily said in the same letter, "Please, Sister, to wait," and she had already written shortly before, "Take faithful care of the dear health and flee no sudden day from your dependent Emily." But it was she who fled. Early in the spring of 1886, after a long winter of illness, she reached out to her old friend seeking "to obtain those constancies which exalt friends." She ended the letter, which proved to be the last, "Emily and Vinnie give the love greater every hour."

SAMUEL BOWLES

"The most triumphant Face"

"March is the Month of Expectation," Emily Dickinson said in one of her poems. While she never described him so, Samuel Bowles must have resembled her favorite month. Like the March weather, he could be as tender as the first foretaste of spring, or suddenly sharp and irritating. He had a driving force within him as strong as the "savage Air" in which she rejoiced. She said of him after his death, "His nature was Future."

The third Samuel Bowles in a succession that carried the name through five generations, he brought acclaim to the name he had inherited. His father, a printer, had come up the Connecticut River from Hartford as a young married man, to start a weekly newspaper dedicated to the principles of Jeffersonian democracy, as represented by what was then called the Republican Party. When *The Springfield Republican* was launched in 1824, its founder carried on the functions of reporter, editor, and printer. On the side he maintained a job-printing business.

His wife, who, like himself, was of good pioneer stock, had the character necessary for conducting the thrifty home of a man who had his own way to make. They had five children, of whom the first died in infancy and the second, a girl, lived to marry but died in early womanhood. Samuel, the third child, born in 1826, was never very strong, and as a boy had so little vitality in his long slender body that he never enjoyed the rough sports of his schoolmates and found it difficult to do his share of the manual labor at home. Springfield was still a country town, with open fields behind the houses, and to lead the family cow to pasture was the job best suited to the growing boy whose interest lay chiefly in books. He had the good fortune to be able to attend a private school for both sexes, conducted by a Mr. Eaton, where he was not only well grounded in mathematics, English, and Latin, but taken on country walks that stimulated his love of nature. His father's failure to see why he should go to college if he were not to be a professional man, was a painful disappointment that left him throughout his life with a sense of lack in his equipment for the place he filled.

Sam started work in his father's office at seventeen with no special enthusiasm for the printing business, but with well-formed habits of industry. It was not long, however, before his imagination was kindled by the possibilities he saw in the little newspaper that already had its steady public. In 1844, when he was eighteen years old, he proposed to his father that the weekly *Republican* should be expanded into a daily paper. Such an undertaking had not occurred to the older Samuel, who was more industrious than daring, but he responded to the boy's persuasions by placing the responsibility for the new venture squarely on his shoulders. The youth's acceptance was characteristic of the man who throughout his life met every challenge with an expenditure of energy that took all his powers.

The Springfield Daily Republican started at a time of rapid expansion in the life of the country. In the 1840's settlers in great numbers were pushing westward. Railroads were being built wherever public opinion was strong enough to make funds available, so that a network of short independent lines was developing in various parts of the country. It was not long before the telegraph began to bring the news from distant places on the day events occurred. Political issues were hot, and were avidly discussed wherever men gathered. It was a time of great agitation by the Abolitionists, and Daniel Webster's oratory was the force depended on by the Whigs to keep the Union secure. In the early years of the daily *Republican*, it supported the Whigs, and backed Webster in his fight to preserve the Union against secession by the South. Young Sam Bowles, during the period of his initiation into journalism, plunged deeply into the political whirlpool, and learned to think for himself on the issues to which he tried to give a fair hearing. The man and his newspaper grew up together. From a single sheet of four pages, containing only two columns of original matter, in a few years the *Republican* expanded to equal the established city papers in size, coverage, and editorial quality. It was largely the creation of one man, whose gifts developed as necessity brought them into use.

The force Sam expended too lavishly at the start gave out before the daily paper had completed one year of life. He became ill, and was sent South to recover. While there fifteen articles on Southern life which he sent back called the subscribers' attention to the young man and his writing and broadened the scope of the paper. On his return he took up responsibility with renewed vigor, and moved steadily forward for some years. At twenty-two he married Mary Schermerhorn of Geneva, New York, whom he had known at school while she was living with her grandfather, James Dwight, in Springfield. The stabilizing influence of a devoted wife led him to say years later to a young man who asked him how he had achieved his success, "I married early, and I worked with all my might."

Mary Bowles outlived her husband by fifteen years, but through the first two decades of their married life she bore seven children that lived and three that were born dead, suffering, meanwhile, from occasional severe attacks of asthma. Her husband seems to have thought of himself as a happily married man, and doubtless the relation was happy up to the limits of the wife's capacities. He was unwaveringly loyal, and he depended for peace of mind on the smoothly running machinery of the household Mrs. Bowles controlled. As husband and wife they started with a background of equality in education and simple good breeding — though Mary's family had more affluence and prestige — but experience developed Sam's sympathies and interests far beyond those of his wife. His boyhood of quiet industry had given little indication of the brilliant mind and ardent spirit that were freed by the hard life of journalism and the far-reaching contacts with the larger world that resulted from his professional associations. Although his highly sensitive nervous system required quiet and solitude, he was irresistibly drawn to people of all sorts. He enjoyed the company of farmers and senators, lawyers and livery-stablemen. He was not analytical in his interest in people, nor did he see them with the eyes of a philanthropist. He simply liked human beings, both men and women, in all the variety of aspects in which they appeared. He could be equally cordial to those who shared his views and to those whom he met in mortal combat in the field of public affairs. The keenness of his judgments developed as he grew with the paper, and after the great shift in American politics that brought the Republican party into being in 1856, his paper became independent of political partisanship and based its policies on the editor's own views of current issues.

Such a personal relation existed between the newspaper and its editor that the atmosphere in the office was somewhat autocratic, but as new members of the staff were added, an attitude of mutual respect kept the wheels running smoothly. If the chief was irritable, it was laid to his wretchedly weak digestion. He expected the best of himself and no less of everyone else, but his own modesty gave him a genuine sympathy with human weakness that often surprised those who had failed to live up to his hopes. The closeness of the creator to the institution he had created is clearly demonstrated by an episode that occurred in 1857. Already well known as the editor of a paper that had reached the front rank of American journals, Bowles, at thirty-one, had an opportunity to take what seemed to be an even larger place in his profession. Three Boston papers, under the leadership of the *Traveller*, proposed to merge and carry on a newspaper of larger scope. When he was asked to take charge, it was with characteristic quickness of decision that he accepted the offer. Placing the *Republican* in the hands of his principal associate, Dr. Holland, he left his family in Springfield while he undertook the initial task of organizing the new paper. The experiment was a failure, and he resigned after four months of frustrated effort to meet the demands of the owners of the three component papers while still holding his own work and that of his staff to the uncompromising standards he could not relinquish. He returned to Springfield to spend the rest of his life where he was free to be himself, and where his own career and that of his paper could expand naturally.

How the friendship between Samuel Bowles and the Dickinsons began one can only speculate. There were many opportunities for the publisher and editor-in-chief of the *Springfield Republican* to meet the people of Amherst. He liked to cover the Amherst College commencement himself, and Edward Dickinson's annual reception brought to the house many of the visitors from out of town. The introduction may have come through Dr. Holland, for the Hollands knew the Dickinsons several years before there is any evidence that Mr. and Mrs. Bowles were acquainted with them.

The friendship that developed was primarily an individual one between Austin Dickinson and the dynamic creator of the paper to which both the Dickinson houses subscribed. The relation of the two men was steady and close for many years, and formed the foundation for the relations of Sam

Bowles with the other members of the family. There is little doubt that Austin counted him as his closest friend. Living all his life in one place, where his professional work as a lawyer and his interests in the college and town never took him very far afield, Austin had no such wide range of acquaintance as Sam enjoyed. Even though Mr. Bowles had other friends on close and familiar terms, it is certain that there was something of special value for him too in this association. From the intense grind of daily newspaper work and the excitement of political battle in which he was often deeply engaged, he found relief in Austin's loyal affection and the more leisurely atmosphere in which he lived. It was not only the relaxation of the talk of horses and gardens, of pictures and books, in which they were both interested, but the freedom to speak from the heart that gave their friendship vitality. An uncritical acceptance on both sides extended to Austin's wife, Sue, and since in the decade following Austin's marriage relations were close between the two Dickinson houses, Emily and Vinnie were included in the group.

The large number of letters from Sam Bowles that Austin and Sue preserved testifies to the warmth of feeling they had for him. Since most of them were not dated by the writer, there is no certainty that the collection is complete, for there are gaps in time that are not covered in the present dating, but much can be told of the development of intimacy between them by the tone of those that remain from the earlier years. The correspondence seems to have begun in 1858. In that year and the next the address was formal, the letters to Austin beginning "My dear Sir." Frequent visits between

Springfield and Amherst ripened the acquaintance, and by 1860 first names had come into use, including those of Emily and Vinnie, who, however, never reciprocated.

In spite of the increasing familiarity between the households in 1860, fewer letters can be dated in that year, possibly because Mr. Bowles and his newspaper were intensely involved in the political excitement that followed the affair of John Brown. The families were aware of each other's activities, however, for Sam wrote to Austin to let him know when he was leaving to attend the Republican national convention in Chicago, and later reported that he had returned in a state of collapse.

In 1861 the exchange of letters and visits reached a high point. In June of that year the Austin Dickinsons' first child, Ned, was born. Sam Bowles, already the father of three children, showed a hearty interest in the occasion, and arranged to send Sue the nurse who had taken care of his wife. He was able to write with feeling of the joys and trials that were ahead of them.

With the increasing intimacy a problem came into the open that was bound to affect the course of the relationship between the two families. There was complete freedom between the two men, but Mary Bowles proved unable to form a parallel friendship with Sue. The latter, whose personality was capable of producing a crushing effect on other women, seems to have intimidated Mary into a state of self-defense that caused a breach of good manners. A touch of jealousy may have been mingled with her sense of inadequacy, for Sue's clever tongue and personal attraction charmed and stimulated those who gathered around her. Sensitive to discord, and honest in acknowledging its cause, the disappointed husband wrote to his host, after a highly uncomfortable visit, a letter of apology instinct with the delicacy that was characteristic of his personal relations. There is no allusion to any provocation on the part of the hostess, and in his plea for a gentle judgment of his own wife, he took on himself the charge of having failed to lead her as she wished him to do, when in her lack of self-reliance she turned defense into offense.

Mrs. Bowles's temperamental difficulty, combined with her fecundity, which kept her at home most of the time, placed her loyal husband in a difficult position. His active mind and warmly responsive emotional nature would have starved without some outside source of sustenance. He needed not only masculine but feminine society, and he succeeded in forming close friendships with several women. The time and place in which he lived favored such relations, for women of his class were beginning to assert their individuality, and at the same time were protected by the accepted view that human beings were made of separate elements that could be designated as "carnal" and "spiritual." Women of the type who interested him — intellectual, articulate, yet possessing feminine charm — simply lived above suspicion. Even a little light flirtation was permissible, since the absolute barriers were recognized on both sides.

Mary Bowles's defeat at the hands of Sue gave a new turn to Sam's friendship with the Austin Dickinsons. It was tacitly acknowledged that they were peculiarly his, though she oc-

casionally invited them to her house when some special event
brought them to Springfield. On her own ground, and when
she was in good health, Mary was hospitable to her husband's
friends. As time went on, he wrote as often to Sue as to
Austin, and concerned himself with her errands in Boston or
New York. In his feeling for them there seems to have been
no loss of affection for either when in later years their marriage was growing precarious. He treated Sue with gallantry,
sometimes with flattery, but was also capable of giving her
brotherly frankness of expression. She was in no danger of
misinterpreting his admiration, for he expressed just as freely
his enthusiasm for her sister, Martha Gilbert Smith, and for
her friend Kate Turner, whom he often met at her house.

At the same time that the pleasant relation with Sue was
developing, an even more important friendship began to take
shape between Sam Bowles and a cousin of his wife's, Maria
Whitney of Northampton. Miss Whitney, one of a large and
notable family, including professors at Harvard and Yale,
seems to have divided her life between intellectual pursuits
and acceding to the demands put upon spinsters to "help out"
in the families of their relatives. She was called in to act as
companion to Mary Bowles late in 1861, when the latter, to
ward off the danger of losing still another child, went to New
York to be under the care of a noted physician when her
next infant was due. The baby, Charles, lived, and two years
later the same program was carried out when Dwight was
born. After that, Maria was often a member of the Bowles
household, where she held the place of aunt to the children,
lightened their mother's responsibilities, and provided their

father with intellectual companionship. When she went west in 1864, to join her geologist brother Josiah in California, Sam Bowles, writing to Sue in apology for the mood she had found him in when she spent a day in Springfield, said of Maria:

> Perhaps Maria's late going had something to do, as you thought, with the day's depression, but it would have been a day of torture & blueness, anyway. Her going has been a trial to me, but I should be unworthy the rich gift of her fresh friendship did I allow it to blue my life, weaken the tide of its flow, or poison the sweetness of its expression. Her gifts to me are too great & noble to be spoiled by such unworthiness. They have been inspiration to every duty, courage for every trial, purity for every thought & deed; new power to struggle against my ill health, new richness & purity & generosity to every friendship; new incentive & strength for every self-sacrifice. I am sure to be the better friend to you & Austin, the better husband & father, the better man in every way, for the inspiration & strength of her example & her words.

After Maria's return she spent a year with the Bowles family, during which she wrote to her brother, William Dwight Whitney, in New Haven of her distress over the gossip that had reached her ears of Mrs. Bowles's jealousy of her. Whether or not there was any truth in the rumor, her relations with the family were not broken, and when she took the eldest daughter, Sallie, to Europe for two years, Mr. Bowles and his son Sam joined them in the summer of 1870. To the end of his life Maria Whitney was counted on for moral support and mental stimulus. She never married, but made a life of her own as a teacher of languages, first in private classes, then at the newly opened Smith College. She

gradually became a member of the circle that centered at
the Austin Dickinsons', but it was not until after the death
of the man whose friendship they had shared that she and
Emily became close friends.

The place that Samuel Bowles filled in the life of Emily
Dickinson cannot be clearly defined, though the high value
he held for her is plainly seen in all she wrote to him and
about him. The nature of their relation remains as elusive as
her friendship with Higginson was categorical. One hesitates
to search it too closely, lest the essence be missed in a confu-
sion of detail. Using her letters to him and his to Austin and
Sue as the principal source, there is still much that must remain conjectural. Since both writers left their letters largely
undated, the task of creating a connected chronology is hindered by hazards that no amount of scholarly labor can overcome. Accidental groupings may produce an effect that is
far from the truth, and within the range of handwriting
variations, which provide an important means of dating,
there is still room for varying interpretation of the allusions
the letters contain. As one of the few friends who received
and kept many letters from Emily Dickinson, however,
Samuel Bowles cannot escape the scrutiny of those who try
to trace the emotional pattern of her life and mind. It is evident, indeed, when one reads the letters she wrote him in
their approximate order, that in the course of twenty years
their friendship passed through several phases, though her
admiration and delight in his personality remained constant.
The greatest intensity in their correspondence coincides

with the period of emotional crisis Emily passed through in the early 1860's. If the letters of those years are read as a chronicle of a life, rather than as separate literary curiosities, the involvement of Samuel Bowles in some way cannot be overlooked. Certain readers will be convinced that he filled the role of the man who, as tradition declares and the love poems indicate, took a central place in the inner drama of that time. Outwardly there is much that would qualify him for that position, for he was near her own age, possessed warmth and wit and charm, and as her brother's friend gave her ample opportunity to become well acquainted with him.

Emily's search for the supreme values in her life led her into different relationships with several men. Five years before she met Samuel Bowles, her first "preceptor," Ben Newton, had died. Afterwards she had initiated a correspondence with Dr. Wadsworth, whom she later called her "shepherd," and described after his death as her "closest earthly friend." The first of these friendships seems to have been primarily intellectual; the second, during the nearly thirty years of its duration, was by her own account mainly on the spiritual level. So far as one is able to follow her relations through her letters, the next friendship to develop was with Bowles, and four years after she first met him she began her correspondence with Higginson. The possibility of the existence of one more correspondent must be considered in connection with the rough drafts of three highly emotional letters to an unnamed "Master" (see p. 49). It is possible that they were addressed — if only to relieve the anguish they express, and laid away in her drawer — to Dr. Wadsworth or to Mr.

Bowles, but certain allusions in them are inconsistent with what is known of either man.

The second and third letters, which were closely tied with the crisis of 1861 and 1862, seem to have been intended for someone at a distance. She asks if he would like to come to New England if he could, and whether, if their positions were reversed, he could forget her "in fight, or flight – or the foreign land." It is true that Bowles was often engaged in verbal "fight" through the columns of his paper, and that he might be said to have taken flight when he went to Europe in the spring of 1862. On the other hand, when Emily asked with seeming hesitation, "Could you come to New England – [this summer – could] would you come to Amherst – Would you like to come – Master?" it was not likely that she was directing her questions to a man whose home was in New England, and who would certainly visit Amherst when he returned in the autumn. It is equally hard to believe that she was thinking of the Reverend Charles Wadsworth, whom she later described as "so noble . . . so fathomless – so gentle," when she implied that the man she loved might forget her, not only in "flight" but in "fight." Since she wrote at the time of the Civil War, it is possible that she was alluding quite literally to battle.

Another puzzling allusion is found in a letter to the Reverend Edward S. Dwight, the recently resigned pastor of the Dickinsons' church, to whom she wrote on January 2, 1862, to explain how she had placed a letter to him in the wrong envelope, sending him meanwhile a poem intended for another friend. She described the other correspondent as "the friend who loves me – and thinks me larger than I am," adding that the verse was meant "to reduce a Glamour, innocently caused." Neither this situation nor the "familiar address" she said she had used, and which she feared had "surprised" the clergyman's "taste," seems in accord with her outward relations with any of her known friends. In the letters from her that Mr. Bowles kept, covering all the years of their friendship, she addressed him no more familiarly than she did Dr. Dwight himself, with an undifferentiated "Dear friend."

Such small discrepancies make it easy to postulate the existence of a man who came into her life for only a short time. Since most of her poems written in the first person seem to be based on her own experience, a poem in the writing of 1872, ten years after the crisis, can be interpreted as an allusion to such a man.

> Somewhere upon the general Earth
> Itself exist Today –
> The Magic passive but extant
> That consecrated me –
>
> Indifferent Seasons doubtless play
> Where I for right to be –
> Would pay each Atom that I am
> But Immortality –
>
> Reserving that but just to prove
> Another Date of Thee –
> Oh God of Width, do not for us
> Curtail Eternity!

It is possible that this poem was written several years earlier, but the content implies that when it was composed a number of years already had elapsed since the separation had occurred. There was no time in the intervening years when Emily did not know where Dr. Wadsworth was living, and, in spite of frequent absences in Europe and the West, Bowles was in constant touch with the Dickinsons. The poem strongly suggests that the person alluded to had disappeared completely from her knowledge.

When Emily first became acquainted with Sam Bowles, he was a young man of thirty-two, tall and handsome, with strikingly expressive dark eyes and a lively manner, whose personality found in her a ready response. He made no claims as a judge of poetry, for his taste in books was entirely unpredictable, and he left all the literary features of the *Republican* in the hands of Dr. Holland. It could not be wholly a matter of chance, however, that the first year of their acquaintance was also the year when Emily made her first packets of carefully copied poems, and probably started seriously to work on them. Mr. Bowles's presence alone, apart from any encouragement he might have given her, would have been a stimulus to her imagination, for the quickness of his mind and the vigor and color of his speech set the tone of the conversation in any company that he found at all congenial to him.

The first visit that Mr. and Mrs. Bowles made to the Austin Dickinsons seems to have been in June 1858. Emily wrote to them afterward, "Dear friends, I am sorry you came, because you went away. Hereafter I will pick no Rose, lest it fade or prick me. I would like to have you dwell here." It is evident that from the beginning it was *Mr.* Bowles she meant, for, in spite of the plural form of the address, she later refers, perhaps inadvertently, to "you and Mrs Bowles." As the friendship progressed, she continued to try to include Mary, but since she shared with her little but a love of flowers, there was no basis for a close relation between them. Later, the tenuous tie ceased to hold, though Emily's courtesy never failed. A letter she wrote to Mary in the summer of 1861, several months after the unfortunate visit that had caused Sam so much pain, gently tries to probe the long silence between them. Emily's delicacy may have been too subtle to be understood, but her concluding sentences are simple and appealing: "I brought my own – myself, to you and Mr Bowles. Please remember me, because I remember you – Always."

During the first two or three years of the friendship, the letters and poems Emily sent were divided about equally between husband and wife. Then, in October and November 1861, a new phase in their relations opened, when Mr. Bowles, whose health had begun to be seriously affected by the intensity of his life and work, spent several weeks at a water-cure establishment in Northampton. Since he had his favorite horse, Pone, with him, he made frequent trips to Amherst, only seven miles away. At this time Emily was going through what she described to Mr. Higginson the following spring as "a terror since September." On one of the occasions when Mr. Bowles called, she refused to see him, and the following day she wrote in explanation:

Perhaps you thought I did'nt care – because I stayed out, yesterday,

I *did* care, Mr Bowles. I pray for your sweet health – to "Alla" – every morning – but something troubled me – and I knew you needed light – and air – so I did'nt come. Nor have I the conceit that you *noticed* me – but I could'nt bear that you, or Mary, so gentle to me – should think me forgetful – It's little, at the most – we can do for our's, and we must do that – flying – or our things are *flown!* Dear friend, I wish you were well –

It grieves me till I cannot speak, that you are suffering. Wont you come back? Cant I bring you something? My little Balm might be *o'erlooked* by wiser eyes – you know – Have you tried the Breeze that swings the Sign – or the Hoof of the Dandelion? *I* own 'em – Wait for *mine!*

This is all that I have to say – Kinsmen need say nothing – but "Swiveller" may be sure of the

"Marchioness."

Emily could hardly have chosen a more abjectly humble figure with which to identify herself than the nameless little slavey from *The Old Curiosity Shop*, whom the facetious Dick Swiveller took pity on, and whose devoted care later saved his life. Even in fun, Mr. Bowles might have had difficulty in seeing himself in the role of the theatrical Dick, but the implication of a servile devotion could hardly be missed.

Meanwhile, between the treatments at the sanatorium, Bowles was driving out in the afternoons to see the country around Northampton, accompanied by Maria Whitney and a friend, sending books to Sue and Kate Turner, and inviting the latter to see the sights of the country town some day when Mr. Dickinson was driving over on business. Nothing is said of Emily in his letters to his wife or to Austin and Sue, but her apology for not seeing him once when he called indicates that she was usually a part of the group. After he left to ac-company Mary to New York where she was to await the birth of the baby Charles, Emily wrote: "It grieves us – that in near Northampton – we have now – no friend – and the old-foreigner-look blurs the Hills – *that* side – " The pleasant weeks at Northampton had been only temporarily helpful, and the symptoms returned. The strain of years of overwork on his sensitive organism made it impossible to effect a quick recovery, and before spring it became obvious that something more drastic would have to be done. Since the great remedy for nervous ailments in those days was a change of scene, he decided to go to Europe for six months, leaving Mary and the children in Springfield, and placing the paper once more in the hands of Dr. Holland and his business associate, Mr. Bryan. He sailed on April 9, 1862.

During the months between Mr. Bowles's sojourn in Northampton and his departure for Europe, Emily wrote him a series of specially intense letters. Only the first and the last two before he sailed can be dated with accuracy, but the con-tents of those between, together with the similarity in hand-writing, seem to bring them naturally together. Emily was suffering from a deep distress that appears, though in dif-ferent ways, in all. The first letter, written in January, says, "Are you willing? I am so far from Land – To offer *you* the cup – it might some Sabbath come *my* turn – Of wine how solemn – full!" There is no explanation of what she is asking when she writes "Are you willing?" but two months later she sent another request that implies she had been sending him letters to be addressed and forwarded to another friend. Substituting her brother's name for her own, in a form of dissemblance that she assumes will be understood because it has been done before, she says,

Dear friend.

Will you be kind to *Austin* – again? And would you be kinder than sometimes – and put the name – on – too – He tells me to tell you – He could not thank you – Austin is disappointed – He expected to see you – today –

He is sure you wont go to Sea – without first speaking to Him. I presume if Emily and Vinnie knew of his writing – they would entreat Him to ask you – not . . .

Austin hopes his errand will not tire you.

The letters of that winter are keyed to the tone of gratitude for the great kindness Mr. Bowles has shown her. In one of them she says, "I cant thank you any more – You are thoughtful so many times, you grieve me *always – now*," but she is never explicit as to the nature of his thoughtful acts.

Three notes of a somewhat different character, apparently related to one another, seem to have been written during the same winter. The difficulty of finding exact dates for the letters that are not tied to some event or other identifying circumstance forces us to take care that we do not push the implications too far. Slight differences in the handwriting of these three could stretch the dates from 1861 to 1863, yet all could have been written in 1862. If they were sent in the order now given, and at that time, they lead to one of two conclusions. The three form a sequence of special emotional intensity when read together, for they appear to be a dramatic confession of love. It is impossible to tell from the veiled wording whether the love Emily acknowledges is for the man to whom she is writing or whether she is confiding in him her love for another.

Both in content and in striking similarities of phrase, these notes are closely connected with the later two of the "Master" letters. This is especially true of the first. Not included among the letters sent to Mrs. Todd for publication in the 1894 edition of letters, it finally came to light so badly damaged that many words have had to be reconstructed, and a few remain uncertain.

Dear friend.
   If I amaze[d] your kindness – My Love is my only apology. To the people of "Chillon" – this – is enoug[h] I have met – no othe[rs.] Would you – ask le[ss] for your *Queen* – M[r] Bowles?
   Then – I mistake – [my] scale – To Da[?] 'tis *daily* to be gran[ted] and not a "Sunday Su[m] [En]closed – is my [d]efence –
   [F]orgive the Gills that ask for Air – if it is harm – to breathe!
   To *"thank" you* – [s]hames my thought!

> [Sh]ould you but fail [at] – Sea –
> [In] sight of me –
> [Or] doomed lie –
> [Ne]xt Sun – to die –
> [O]r rap – at Paradise – unheard
> I'd *harass God*
> Until he let [you] in!

Emily.

In the "Master" drafts Emily called herself "Daisy" — her name for the small, humble, rustic person she felt herself to be in relation to the godlike being of the lover. In the letter to Bowles the mutilated word "Da" may stand for the same name. In one of the drafts she says "if I wish with a might I cannot repress – that mine were the Queen's place – the love

of the Plantagenet is my only apology." The letter to Bowles
refers to "your Queen," and declares, "My Love is my only
apology." In both draft and letter "Chillon" is used to express
the imprisoned feeling that life had given her.

Next in the series comes the poem "Title divine – is mine!"
with a short note at the end:

> Here's – what I had to "tell you" –
> You will tell no other? Honor – is it's own pawn –

She implies that she had seen Mr. Bowles recently, but had
failed to have a private conversation with him, as she had
hoped. She wanted to confide in him the full extent of her
commitment to the man she loved.

His reply evidently showed some alarm, for she wrote again
to reassure him, using a poem once more to convey her message.

Dear friend

If you doubted my Snow – for a moment – you never will – again –
I know –
Because I could not say it – I fixed it in the Verse – for you to read –
when your thought wavers, for such a foot as mine –

> Through the strait pass of suffering –
> The Martyrs – even – trod.
> Their feet – upon Temptation –
> Their faces – upon God –
>
> A stately – shriven – Company –
> Convulsion – playing round –
> Harmless – as streaks of Meteor –
> Upon a Planet's Bond –
>
> Their faith – the everlasting troth –
> Their Expectation – fair –

The Needle – to the North Degree –
Wades – so – thro' polar Air!

The word "snow" in this note seems to carry the same meaning that she gave to "white" when she used it in the earlier
of the two drafts. "What would you do with me if I came 'in
white,' " she wrote, and "I did'nt think to tell you, you did'nt
come to me 'in white,' nor ever told me why,"

No Rose, yet felt myself a'bloom,
No Bird – yet rode in Ether.

Her answer to the erotic approach of a lover, suggested
here, is given in the allusion to symbolic snow. She wanted
Mr. Bowles to understand that her renunciation was complete, and that it had placed her in the company of the mar-
tyrs. In another poem, "Of Tribulation – these are They,"
she had said:

All these – did conquer –
But the Ones who overcame most times –
Wear nothing commoner than Snow –
Or Ornament – but Palms –

The similarities in phrase between the two groups of letters
suggest that they were written to the same person. Possibly
the first letter to Bowles was a final distillation, deemed suitable to send, from the unrestricted private outpouring of the
drafts. Yet Emily often repeated words that had special significance to her at the time, in letters to different people.
Nothing in the other letters she wrote to him, or in those he
wrote to Austin and Sue, gives any ground for the assump-

tion that it was he of whom she said in the draft, "I heard of a thing called 'Redemption' – which rested men and women. You remember I asked you for it – you gave me something else." It seems highly improbable, too, that he was the man to whom she wrote — even though the words remained in her locked drawer — "the knee that bore her once unto [royal] wordless rest." The freedom of his friendships with women was based on his sense of chivalrous propriety. He was not the sort of man to be suddenly moved by a fatherly impulse toward a troubled young woman. There was something in his nature, however, that was almost feminine. The quickness of his responses, the warmth of feeling he was willing to express, his concern for human values in the dilemmas of daily living, would have made him an appealing confidant. If she had revealed to him her love for another man, the terms in which she wrote to him could be accounted for by his being drawn into the aura of her secret, where all was intensified.

If Mr. Bowles received these letters in the present order and in close succession, he could not have failed to find his situation a difficult one. It would be painful to a sensitive man to see a woman he was fond of suffering because of her love for him, or to carry the burden of a secret of such an intimate nature, involving her relations with someone else. Emily asked for nothing but understanding, and, even if she saw him in the central role, she seems to have assumed that his feeling was compassion rather than love. But, as a man whose interests and affections were directly connected with the outside world, he probably found her condition morbid and her emotions overdriven. It is unlikely that his going to Europe had any direct relation to this episode, but the pressure of Emily's intensity may have added to his already great need of relief.

It was only a week after his departure that Emily wrote her first letter to Higginson, asking for his criticism of her verse. When, in her second letter, ten days later, she answered his questions about her age and education, she spoke of her early "tutor" — undoubtedly an allusion to Ben Newton — and added, "Then I found one more – but he was not contented I be his scholar – so he left the Land." It has been generally supposed that she was referring to Dr. Wadsworth, who left Philadelphia in the spring of 1862 to take a new pastorate in San Francisco, but this conclusion seems a little forced, since he did not sail for California until the first of May. Samuel Bowles, however, had already gone before she appealed to Mr. Higginson to assume the role of her new "preceptor."

The complexities of a mind so deeply troubled as Emily's at this time are hard to follow. Her whole being was disturbed, and she probably could not separate the emotional reactions that had to do with her own inner life from those that were related to the people with whom she was concerned. It is possible that the departure of Sam Bowles clarified the situation enough to enable her to see that what she needed then was intellectual leadership to help her cope with the immense flood of creativity that almost overwhelmed her. Although she failed in the end to find in Higginson the support she longed for, his friendly interest meant much in her troubled condition. She told him long afterward that he had saved her life. There is no evidence that with Bowles's departure she had lost a literary critic, but she had been sending him poems for several years, and it seems certain that he had encouraged her. She wrote Higginson, in her second letter, "Two Editors of Journals came to my Father's House, this winter – and asked me for my Mind – and when I asked them 'Why,' they said I was penurious – and they, would use it for the World." One of the editors was certainly Samuel Bowles. Emily must have complied with his request, for on March 1, 1862, she made her first appearance in print, in the *Springfield Republican*. The poem "Safe in their Alabaster Chambers" was published anonymously, under the title "The Sleeping." It is possible that the thanks she poured out to Mr. Bowles that winter reflected not only his understanding of her personal dilemma, but also a poet's gratitude for appreciation.

After he had been gone several months, he wrote in a letter to Susan Dickinson, "When you next write, tell Emily to give me one of her little gems! How does she do this summer!" He would not have written in this vein of friendly interest and concern if he had received the letter addressed to a distant "Master." He preserved two letters which Emily did send him, however, full of personal feeling, but containing no allusions to the fervid agitation of the previous winter. When she said, "Would you please come home?" it was less a demand than an expression of the anxiety she always felt about the safety of her friends. Yet when he returned in November and visited the Dickinsons after Thanksgiving, Emily found herself too much moved to face him. She sent a little note downstairs, saying,

SAMUEL BOWLES

Dear friend

I cannot see you. You will not less believe me. That you return to us alive, is better than a Summer. And more to hear your voice below, than News of any Bird.

Emily.

The habit of withdrawal was becoming so strong that she could not trust herself in such a meaningful encounter. Her family and friends had not yet accepted her seclusion, and as she told Mr. Bowles, in thanking him later for a present he had left for her, Vinnie and Austin "upbraided" her for not going down to welcome their dear friend.

How long she continued to refuse to see him is not clear. Judging by the handwriting, only two of the letters from her that he kept were written in 1863, and neither of them is pointedly personal. One consists of the poem "The Zeros taught us Phosphorus," sent with a brief message at the end, "I could'nt let Austin's note go – without a word." The other was – or purported to be – written on behalf of her mother to accompany a gift of apples. He wrote numerous letters in that year to Austin and Sue, but made no direct statements regarding Emily. In spite of the frequent communications with the house next door, however, there was a shadow over their relations that Bowles seemed to feel keenly, but which, like so much else in his friendship with the Dickinsons, remains ambiguous. It was probably in February of 1863 that he wrote:

I will come up & spend to-morrow with you, by way of Northampton, in the morning, returning by evening train. It is all I can do now. Mary will not come, of course. It could hardly be expected, since

Sue has not been to see her, even though she has been to Springfield two or three times.

After that visit, or another in the same winter, he wrote sensitively of the nuances of feeling he had been aware of while he was in Amherst. It is easy to see that the pressure which the Dickinsons' intensity put on their friends was as strong in the case of Austin as in that of Emily.

My dear Austin,

I give thanks anew for the pleasant day with you. The gift of friendship is a holy one, & its proofs stimulate and sadden, as the most delicate of responsibilities. It annoys me that I cannot do more, write oftener, visit more frequently, & stay longer — as you would wish. — Some of the reasons for my incapacity, & the consequent disappointment to you, you know, because I have told you. — I have many cares & small power. The price of life & health to me is clearly abstinence "from all which does intoxicate" — from work, excitement, even earnest feeling; from irregularities in eating, drinking, & exercise. Sometimes life seems not worth the keeping at such egotistical cost. It would not for self, but we all give bonds that must be respected. — Other causes for my reticence — of which you seem sometimes oppressed, — you ought to know without my explaining. I thought to write you of them fully; but I cannot. You certainly are not ignorant of them. I must respect them: so must you. They are not unconquerable — it has seemed to me the correct thing to put them aside. But that, belongs not to me, nor to you. So long as they exist, however, I pray you to be indulgent to my shortcomings in the duties and delights of friendship.

The reticence that kept Mr. Bowles from being explicit about the "other causes" of his seeming withdrawal from his friend has prevented intrusion upon them. In view of his allusion to Mary and Sue in the letter giving his plans for a visit, it seems probable that their insecure relations had again brought a conflict of loyalties. But oblique references to a problem that belonged to someone else suggest another interpretation. He may have found that his enigmatic relations with Emily had become acutely embarrassing. When he said, "it has seemed to me the correct thing to put them aside," he may have meant that, since he recognized the intense and explosive nature of her feeling for him, it was best to keep at a distance. However, there were two messages to Emily in letters to Austin a little later that show he was in communication with her. The first of these gives the impression that he found her withdrawal, not only from him, but from the world in general, so puzzling that he could only treat it as a whim, to be shocked out of her by light ridicule. At the conclusion of his letter he sent greetings to both households, which included in Austin's home his two younger cousins, the orphaned Newman girls:

To the girls & all hearty thought — Vinnie ditto, — and to the Queen Recluse my especial sympathy — that she has "overcome the world" — Is it really true that they sing "Old Hundred" and "Aleluia" perpetually in Heaven — ask her; and are dandelions, asphodels, & maiden's cross the standard flowers of the etherial?

No response from Emily has been recorded, and it is by no means certain that Austin considered the message one that should be delivered. Some word from her reached Bowles, however, that spring, for he sent her another message in a letter to Austin late in April, parts of which follow:

My dear Austin,

Are you planted & not sprouted yet? I have been looking for you to "come up" these many days. My peas are. But do you wait for rain?

MY FRIENDS ARE MY "ESTATE"

I have been in a savage, turbulent state for some time — indulging in a sort of chronic disgust at everything & everybody — I guess a good deal as Emily feels — & have been trying to garden, too. But I tire out so soon, it is of small use — & then I am gone for the day, & have to wait for the morning to come again . . . . Tell Emily I am here, in the old place. "Can you not watch one hour?"

The mood of this message is in marked contrast to the teasing spirit of the earlier one. No letter from Emily has been preserved to which it can be a response, yet the rebuke implies an importunate demand from her. The assurance that he is "still in the old place" is an acknowledgment of her long reliance on him for meeting some emotional need, but there is no hint as to the nature of it. Perhaps his impatience was due quite as much to his own discouraged state as to Emily's urgency, which may have been no more extreme than in her expressions of anxiety for other friends. The insulation with which she had now surrounded herself must have made her particularly enigmatic, and Bowles had no way of knowing about the changes that were taking place in her. It was only in the poems she was writing at this time that a new trend began away from the outpouring of the emotions that centered in her thwarted love toward a philosophical interpretation of her experience.

The two letters that complete the cycle of their correspondence during Emily's years of crisis show no excessive or morbid feeling on her part, but a freely expressed affection that had grown through the years. Both written in 1864, they are concerned with an exchange of books. She had lent him her copy of the poems of the Brontë sisters, "Currer, Ellis &

Acton Bell," and wrote urging him to keep it. The second
letter shows that he had refused it as a gift, but when he
returned it he seems to have sent her a volume of Mrs.
Browning. She begins the letter:

Dear friend.

How hard to thank you – but the large Heart requites itself. Please
to need me – I wanted to ask you to receive *Mr* Browning – from me –
but you denied my Bronte – so I did not dare – Is it too late – now?
I should like so much, to remind you – how kind you had been to *me*.

You could choose – as you did before – if it would not be ob-
noxious – except where you "measured by *your* heart," you should
measure – *this* time – by *mine*. I wonder which would be biggest!

For the first time in writing to him she concluded the letter,
"Affy, Emily" – a familiarity she used only to those with
whom she felt entirely comfortable. The emphasis is still on
his kindness, but in terms of the past. Whatever subjective
elements she had lodged at his door seem to have been completely withdrawn, and her feeling for this dear friend was
now free to exist on a basis of mutual affection.

As the public figure of Samuel Bowles grew in importance,
the journeys he made took him farther away and held him
longer, so that the friends in Amherst saw less of him. He
had found early in his career that he could not discharge his
responsibility to his readers effectively unless he understood
thoroughly what was being said and done in public affairs.
Telephones did not exist, and telegraphic dispatches were
too meager. The routine work of the paper could be carried
on by others, but as the guiding spirit he had to give part of
his time to being on the spot where events were happening.

He made frequent trips to Boston, to keep up with the politics of the state, and took longer sojourns in Washington, where he talked with the men who were involved in national issues. In spite of his constant fight against fatigue, he enjoyed these outings, the men and women he met, and the new interests they brought him. When he was in New York or Boston he looked over the new books, often buying them for his friends in Amherst, and visited the art galleries. In the 1860's he and Austin both began to collect paintings, which they sometimes lent for local exhibitions. The driving trips he took for relaxation in the Berkshires or the White Mountains fostered his love of nature, and he found that nothing refreshed him so much as days spent out-of-doors. Accordingly, in 1865, when illness again threatened him, he planned to be away for several months, and made an overland journey to California.

The West, at that time, was opening up rapidly. The transcontinental railroad was under construction, but not yet completed, and from Omaha they traveled across the plains and through the mountains by stagecoach. The journey was of immense interest to Bowles and his companions, all men in political life or journalism. Every feature of the new country they covered, in spite of physical discomforts and fatigue endured on the way, brought refreshment and stimulus to Bowles's eager mind. He wrote home detailed accounts of the trip for his paper, which were afterward published in a volume entitled *Across the Continent*. His style was fresh and vivid, and, as always, he tried to give a true picture of what he observed. The West so fascinated him that he took two more trips, in 1868 and 1869, when the railroad was in operation. On the first his eldest daughter, Sallie, accompanied him on a camping trip in the Rocky Mountains, and on the second Mrs. Bowles, whose family was now complete, went with him on an extended tour of Colorado, California, and Oregon.

The correspondence with Austin and Susan continued steadily, but there is no sign of any direct communication between him and Emily, who in those years appears to have written few letters to anyone. It was not until 1874, after a gap of a decade, that another series of letters from her throws light on the last phase of their friendship. His name, however, appears on the fold of a paper containing a poem, in handwriting of about 1870.

> He is alive, this morning –
> He is alive – and awake –
> Birds are resuming for Him –
> Blossoms – dress for His Sake.
> Bees – to their Loaves of Honey
> Add an Amber Crumb
> Him – to regale – Me – Only –
> Motion, and am dumb.
>
> Emily.

This seems to have been written as a note to be given to Mr. Bowles while he was visiting in Amherst, but since it remained among her own papers, it was probably never delivered. The strong feeling that prevented Emily from expressing her delight in his presence except through the picture of nature's own celebration, probably prompted her to withhold it from him.

MY FRIENDS ARE MY "ESTATE"

Three times during the early 1870's Mr. Bowles went to Europe, which had become his refuge when he found himself nearing the end of his endurance. He was fighting battles for honesty and justice in administration. The *Republican* fearlessly exposed the railroad scandals and other social evils of the time, and the publishers were several times involved in lawsuits. The paper's success as an institution was at its height, but the dissension among the partners which led to reorganization in 1872 and financial difficulties in the crash of 1873 wore heavily upon the founder. His now infrequent visits to Amherst were times of relaxation for him and of rejoicing for his friends.

When Edward Dickinson died in June 1874 Samuel Bowles brought the warmth of his tender consideration to the help of the stricken family. Emily wrote to Colonel Higginson, "Mr Bowles was with us – With that exception I saw none." To Bowles himself she wrote, apparently in answer to a letter from him soon after the event:

I should think you would have few Letters for your own are so noble that they make men afraid – and sweet as your Approbation is – it is had in fear – lest your depth convict us.

You compel us each to remember that when Water ceases to rise – it has commenced falling. That is the law of Flood. The last Day that I saw you was the newest and oldest of my life.

Resurrection can come but once – first – to the same House. Thank you for leading us by it.

Come always, dear friend, but refrain from going. You spoke of not liking to be forgotten. Could you, tho' you would? Treason never knew you.

Emily.

He thought of their loneliness on the first Thanksgiving,

sending flowers to Mrs. Dickinson and charging Austin's son
Ned with the responsibility of seeing that they were delivered. He marked the anniversary of Mr. Dickinson's death,
each year, by a call, a note, or a gift of flowers. After seeing
him in 1875, probably on that anniversary, Emily wrote, "If
we die, will you come for us, as you do for Father? 'Not born'
yourself, 'to die,' you must reverse us all." He seemed to her
more intensely alive than anyone else she knew. Probably in
thanks for a photograph of himself he had sent her in the last
year of his life Emily wrote,

Dear friend,
    You have the most triumphant Face out of Paradise – probably be-
cause you are there constantly, instead of ultimately –

> Ourselves – we do inter – with sweet derision
> The Channel of the Dust – who once achieves –
> Invalidates the Balm of that Religion
> That doubts – as fervently as it believes.

Emily.

Emily might have detected a note of "sweet derision" in
Mr. Bowles's speech when she had last seen him, for until
the end he fought the weakening body that refused to carry
his spirit longer in the world he loved so well. He rallied from
a stroke in the summer of 1876, but was again taken ill in
the autumn of 1877. Another stroke in December left him
helpless in body, but active in mind until his death on January 16, 1878.

Writing at once to Mary Bowles, with whom she had not
corresponded for years, Emily said, "To remember our own

Mr Bowles is all we can do. With grief it is done, so warmly and long, it can never be new."

"Our own Mr Bowles" — a different man, perhaps, for each of those who remembered him warmly and long. He did not always form close friendships with his associates, yet he always called out their loyalty. For years there was a barrier of some sort between him and Dr. Holland, which the latter attributed to a difference in temperament, but which from Bowles's point of view may have been the result of his personal distaste for the lay preaching that was so popular with Dr. Holland's readers. Both men, however, had strong gifts of humanity, out of which grew a relationship that brought Mr. Bowles hurrying home from Chicago in 1868 to see the Holland family off for Europe, and ten years later took Dr. Holland from a sickbed to speak at the memorial service for his friend in Springfield. Many persons in high places attended, and gave tribute to the character and achievements of the man whose memory they were honoring, but the men and women who knew him best mourned, as Emily did, for the light that was extinguished when he died.

Among those most deeply affected by the death of Samuel Bowles was Maria Whitney, to whom Emily started writing during their friend's last illness. Miss Whitney was making frequent trips to Springfield, and may have been the messenger between the Bowles and Dickinson houses. In their common sorrow after Bowles's death, Emily wrote her a series of letters that fearlessly recognized the depth of the other woman's devotion. Her perception went deep, and she was not afraid to utter the truth in regard to the emotional life. She implied that to Maria he was — to use her words in the poem "Of all the Souls that stand create" — the "Atom" she "preferred." Even though Miss Whitney deleted passages from the letters when they were published, Emily's recognition of the measure of her loss is still clear in the opening lines of the first: "I have thought of you often since the darkness, – though we cannot assist another's night."

"This is Night – now – but we are not dreaming," Emily had written to Mrs. Holland a few weeks before the death of Samuel Bowles, but when she later remembered her "own Mr Bowles" her feeling for him, which had passed through many phases, was resolved into a glowing appreciation of the whole man. After he was gone from sight she adopted for him what she called "his memorial name," "Mr Sam," in place of the respectful "Mr Bowles" she had always used, for death, in a sense, brought him nearer.

He was no longer the man of heavy responsibilities, making hurried visits to his friends. When he was gone he could be cherished as a priceless possession by those who knew him, and Emily's immense capacity for admiration brought its own compensation for the loss of its object. In her letters to members of his family, to Maria Whitney, to Mrs. Holland, and to Sue, she shared her picture of the man who had always brought her an incomparable sense of life.

To Sue he had been the comradely yet gallant companion, who could be counted on for steady and affectionate interest in all the concerns of his friends, and who brought relief from the boredom of routine life. The effect he had on the group that met in Sue's drawing room is reflected in a letter Emily wrote her when she heard that a biography of their friend was to be written. "You remember," she said, "his swift way of wringing and flinging away a Theme, and others picking it up and gazing bewildered after him, and the prance that crossed his Eye at such times was unrepeatable."

In the spring of 1878 Emily wrote to Mrs. Holland, "It is hard not to hear again that vital 'Sam is coming' —— though if grief is a test of a priceless life, he is compensated. He was not ambitious for redemption — that was why it is his. 'To him that hath, shall be given.' " She referred to his "Arabian presence," and described him as Austin's "Cashmere confederate." Light and color she had always associated with him. Observing his physical frailty, she had written to him in 1875, "Your coming welds anew that strange Trinket of Life, which each of us wear and none of us own, and the phosphorescence of your's startles us for it's permanence." Soon after he was gone, she said in a letter to Mary, "Dear 'Mr. Sam' is very near, these midwinter days. When purples come on Pelham, in the afternoon we say 'Mr. Bowles's colors.' " To Maria Whitney she spoke of him as "Hoarded Mr Samuel" — a treasure to be closely guarded.

But Samuel Bowles was too big a man to be reserved for a private hoard. George Merriam wrote to Austin and Sue to ask for their letters from Sam, and Sue seems to have responded heartily, offering not only her letters and Austin's, but Emily's as well. After receiving her apologies for having made this promise without asking permission, Emily wrote in reply, "I felt it no betrayal, Dear – Go to my Mine as to your own, only more unsparingly – I can scarcely believe that the Wondrous Book is at last to be written, and it seems like a Memoir of the Sun, when the Noon is gone." How it happened that her generous offer never was fulfilled is not known. The two volumes of Merriam's *Life and Times of Samuel Bowles* appeared in 1885 without any of the letters to these intimate friends. It is possible that Sue had undertaken to make selections from them and then failed to put the project through, as she did a few years later when Lavinia asked her help in arranging Emily's poems for publication, or that Austin, feeling that some of the letters were too intimate for publication, had refused his permission. The world lost the opportunity of reading what Samuel Bowles said to Emily Dickinson, for after her death Lavinia destroyed all the letters her sister had saved. Emily would not have offered them if they had contained anything revealingly personal, but they might have thrown light on his attitude toward her, and added substance to the outlines that now are undefined. The ambiguity that pervades their relations in one period of their friendship takes nothing away from the impression of color and richness in the play of their personalities during twenty years of association. Whatever his exact role in Emily's life may have been, the figure of Samuel Bowles in the total picture stands out with special luminosity.

THOMAS WENTWORTH HIGGINSON

"Could you instruct me now?"

The leading article in the April 1862 *Atlantic Monthly* was Thomas Wentworth Higginson's "Letter to a Young Contributor." It was Mr. Higginson's twenty-second contribution to the magazine since his first appearance in its pages in March 1858 with a plea for physical culture, under the title "Saints and their Bodies." He could speak with authority about what editors found acceptable, and his reputation had already brought him numerous letters from literary aspirants.

Putting his potential young contributors at ease by his initial statement that they would meet no prejudice against new or obscure authors, he genially declared, "To take the lead in bringing forward a new genius is as fascinating a privilege as that of the physician who boasted to Sir Henry Halford of having been the first man to discover Asiatic cholera and to communicate it to the public." When genius actually presented itself he seems to have found the privilege as embarrassing as it was fascinating. His excellent practical advice on turning in a neat manuscript, on cutting and smoothing and avoiding high-flown phrases, may have been written as much for the benefit of the editorial staff as for the hopeful writers, but he was an able critic as well as a good teacher, and had himself mastered a style not far removed from the "mode of writing which unites the smoothness of the eighteenth century with the vigor of the seventeenth" for which he felt the age was ready.

For one reader, however, the significance of the article seems to have been summed up in the single phrase, "Charge your style with life," for she responded promptly with the question, "Are you too deeply occupied to say if my verse is alive?" Her undated letter, in an envelope postmarked "April 15" and addressed without title to "T. W. Higginson, Worcester, Mass." was not signed, but the name "Emily Dickinson," written in pencil on a card, was enclosed in a smaller envelope within. Mr. Higginson was thus confronted at once with the elusiveness that continued to baffle him during the entire period of this correspondence. Perhaps the custom, then current, of publishing magazine articles anonymously set a precedent for her which sanctioned this shy compromise. Mr. Higginson's name had not appeared in the magazine that carried his article, but it was customary for the literary columns of the daily papers to announce the contents of the leading magazines and the names of the authors just before the publication date, and Emily Dickinson was a constant reader of the *Springfield Republican*.

According to Higginson's own account in his article "Emily Dickinson's Letters," which appeared in the *Atlantic Monthly* for October 1891, four poems were enclosed with this letter: "Safe in their Alabaster Chambers," "I'll tell you how the Sun rose," "We play at Paste," and "The nearest Dream recedes unrealized." Reflecting many years later on the effect of the letter and its enclosures, Higginson used a figure from the last of these when he said, "The bee himself did not evade the school boy more than she evaded me; and even to this day I still stand bewildered, like the boy."

In seeking a literary adviser, Emily Dickinson could hardly have chosen a man whose temperament and outlook differed more markedly from her own. Although the two had in common the cultural background of their native New England, the teacher accepted it as the heir to a goodly heritage, while his "scholar" thought of New England as the place where she lived and felt at home.

The Boston patrician, completely at home on the intellectual heights sustained by the atmosphere in which he grew up, was of a highly active temperament. As a boy in Cambridge, avid for knowledge, he alternated outdoor adventure with his explorations in books, and before he was sixteen he had built up a rich store of information in diverse fields of learning. His love of nature, gained in early boyhood, remained the great solace of his life. His close observation of its phenomena provided the occasion for many of his earlier essays in the *Atlantic Monthly,* and it was probably through her reading of these that Emily Dickinson became acquainted with his writing and "experienced honor" for him. Yet, even in the delight in flowers and birds which she shared with him there was a marked difference, for her approach to all the things of nature was the subjective one of the artist, while Higginson's attitude was that of a somewhat romantic amateur naturalist.

In human relations these two individuals were equally far apart. While Emily Dickinson clung with ardor to her chosen few and lived to a large degree in solitude, Higginson's responsive and kindly nature led him into easy social contact with numberless men and women. They both loved children, but while Emily allied herself with them and took part in their interests, Higginson's attitude was warmly paternal. A woman who knew him in her childhood remembers him as a man to whom children instinctively ran when they saw him coming in the street.

While Emily sought the hidden sources of human experience, he was concerned with the actions and manners of his own and previous generations. If her business, as she wrote in one of her early letters to him, was "circumference," his extended like the innumerable radii from a fixed center. His rational mind had been given freedom to develop and had received the influence of the best liberal thinkers of the day. Since to study theology was almost mandatory for a young man of high purpose, he followed this course, though with somewhat fluctuating convictions. He became a Unitarian minister, but the two pulpits he occupied — in Newburyport and then in Worcester — were those of independent, "free" churches. No parish life could long contain the energies of so expansive a nature. His inborn sense of justice, served by his love of action, led him to take part in movements for the benefit of special classes, or for the improvement of society in general. His participation in the abolitionist movement was no matter of mere speechmaking, for he engaged in violent action in the cases of two fugitive slaves in Boston, and took a leading part in the attempt to free John Brown. A cause that was equally near his heart and of longer duration was the woman suffrage movement. Among his papers there is a copy of a circular announcing a meeting in 1869 to organize a national association for woman's suffrage, on which his signature appears with those of Lucy Stone, Caroline Severance, his life-long friend Julia Ward Howe, and George H. Vibbert.

Higginson's special interest in the problems of women extended far beyond the question of their right to vote. The Victorian attitude elevating women to a place apart was transformed by him into an admiration which championed their right to a more abundant life on every side. Perhaps his devotion and patience in caring for an invalid wife through most of the thirty years of his first marriage found compensation in fostering the activity of other women who were more fortunate. He became the apostle of the normal and the natural, advocating physical training for women equal to — though not necessarily identical with — that granted their brothers. Except for one intense friendship with a fellow-student during his years at Harvard, his chosen companions seem to have been women more often than men. It was natural that young women of talent should turn to him for advice, and before Emily Dickinson opened her correspondence with him he had already had a number of protégées, the best known of whom was Harriet Prescott Spofford. One suspects that he occasionally mistook charm for genius, and fostered some ambitions that were based less on originality of mind than on the ability to write smooth English.

It could not have been easy for a man of Higginson's type of mind to evaluate the life and genius of Emily Dickinson. Her writing denied his standards of form and style; she deliberately refused the privileges for freedom and action he wished to bestow on her sex; she hid behind a veil of glittering words and failed to become manifest as flesh and blood. Even after a correspondence of seven years he could not believe in the reality of her desire for solitude. "You must come down to Boston sometime," he wrote, "All ladies do." He was unable to conceive of a woman of talent and intelligence who did not wish to mingle with her kind. She did not fit into any compartment of his world, yet she possessed a power that astonished and plagued him. When, after eight years of baffled and intermittent effort to understand her, he went to see her at her own home, he was nervously exhausted from the effort to meet the pull of her strangely magnetic personality. To the women who were closest to him, his wife and sisters, he could explain her only as "partially insane," "cracked," or "singular." Yet, she had placed such confidence in him and maintained such loyalty as years went by that his benevolent nature responded with puzzled protectiveness, mingled with a genuine though somewhat reluctant sense of fascination.

In the beginning, however, Emily was to Higginson merely an oddity chance had thrown in his way. On the day after he had received her first letter he added a postscript to a letter he was writing to James T. Fields, then editor of the *Atlantic Monthly*: "I foresee that 'Young Contributors' will send me worse things than ever now. Two such specimens of verse as came yesterday and the day before fortunately not for pub-lication." The following day he wrote to his mother, "Since that Letter to a Young Contributor I have more wonderful effusions than ever sent me to read with request for advice, which is hard to give. Louise was quite overwhelmed with two which came in two successive days." One of these he quoted; although it was not one of Emily Dickinson's, he gave no recognition to the superior quality of the verses he had received from her the same day. There is no record of his first impression of them except this telling omission, yet his curi-osity seems to have been sufficiently aroused to induce him to answer her letter almost at once, for it was only ten days after the receipt of the first that a second letter from her arrived.

Taking from his article a figure he had elaborated on cloth-ing one's thought with words, she confessed her inability to judge her own "thoughts in the gown." Although Higginson advised young readers to "roll" their thought "into one good English word," his own image had been expanded into ninety-six words, while Emily's was contained in a single phrase. She made further acknowledgment of his article by referring to Ruskin, whom he had quoted, and to Sir Thomas Browne, the vigor of whose style he recommended. In answer to his inquiry regarding her age she stated that she had written only one or two poems before the past winter. This statement re-flects a changed attitude toward her writing, however, rather than an actual fact, for she had nearly three hundred poems put away in her drawer before the beginning of 1862. She explained that she had recently begun to work seriously, under the stress of some severe emotional disturbance. With a new critical attitude she had probably rejected some of her earlier work, choosing the few that she felt were worthy of remembrance.

Emily's answers to the questions Mr. Higginson had asked threw enough light on her personality to enable him to read her poems with more insight and to see in them something of the living quality in regard to which she so longed to be assured. He was now interested enough to offer her advice, to which she responded with a series of letters showing her gratitude on one hand and the resistance on the other that was to characterize the relation for years to come.

Unable to resist Emily's touching pleas for his guidance, which to modern ears sound somewhat coy, Mr. Higginson shouldered the task assigned him, but found himself unable to criticize the verses without knowing more of the person who had written them. He asked for her photograph, but received in reply a description of her appearance and an outline of their future relations. Such intellectual loneliness as she hinted at must have been inconceivable to a man who had the power to choose his companions among the best minds of his day, and her attitude toward him as shown in the question "Are you perfectly powerful?" must have roused the champion in him to her aid.

She sent him more poems. "Are these more orderly?" she asked demurely, describing the devastating effects of her efforts to organize her work, and enclosing verses even farther removed from the prescription of the "preceptor" than the earlier ones had been. In answer to his charge that she confessed the little mistake but omitted the large, she sent him verses full of dissonances and containing such startling irregularities of syntax as "among my mind," a phrase that must have jarred unpleasantly "among" the mind of her critic. On Emily's side, however, the progress of the relationship is marked by the changes in signature. With the second letter she had overcome her shyness sufficiently to sign herself "Your friend, E. Dickinson." In the fourth she called herself "Your Scholar," a title that appeared intermittently at first, but was repeated more consistently the farther the friendship became removed from that of teacher and pupil.

Several letters passed between them during the spring and early summer of 1862, before Mr. Higginson's participation in the Civil War caused an interruption in the correspondence. From the beginning of the war, more than a year before, he had been intensely interested in its events and deeply identified with the Union cause. In the first months of the conflict he had framed a plan to bring troops from Kansas, and under the leadership of John Brown, Jr., to launch a campaign through Pennsylvania, but the governor of that state failed to approve it. With the extension of operations in the spring of 1862 the question of his own enrollment for military service began to concern him. As a minister and the husband of an invalid, the matter involved serious conflicts for him, and it is not strange if he occasionally delayed in answering the letters of his unpredictable correspondent. On August 15, he wrote to his mother, "I have obtained authority to enlist a military company for nine months. I go as captain . . . It seemed to me also . . . that beyond a certain point one has no right to concentrate one's whole life on one private duty. Mary will make the best of it as she always does & will either go to Boston if I can find suitable accommodation or stay here." In September he joined his company in barracks at Worcester. Emily's letter written in July probably remained unanswered, and nearly three months later, in an envelope postmarked October 6, came an anxious inquiry from her: "Did I displease you, Mr. Higginson? But won't you tell me how? Your friend, E. Dickinson."

Mr. Higginson's courtesy would certainly have prompted a reply to this appeal if he could possibly have found the time for it, but there is nothing to show that Emily received an explanation of his silence. It was not until the following spring that her next letter was written. She had found "by accident" that he had gone, probably some time after the event. Early in November, as his regiment was about to leave for the South, he had received a commission to command a regiment of freed slaves in South Carolina, and left hurriedly to join his troops at Fort Saxton. He threw himself heartily into his work, becoming teacher, guardian, and friend to the simple souls under his command, and coming close to the conflict only in a few minor engagements during the year and a half of his service. In retrospective mood he wrote in his diary in 1875, "I never was happier than when in the army, entirely absorbed in active duties." This view of military life contrasted sharply with Emily's picture of it when she wrote in April 1863, "War feels to me an oblique place," and entreated him, if he could do so with honor, to avoid death.

Injured by a blow on the side from a fragment of shell or a splinter of wood during a raid for "contraband" recruits, Colonel Higginson's health became so much affected by what had appeared at first to be a mere bruise that he was obliged to leave the army in the spring of 1864. Emily heard the news and, concerned for his health, wrote a letter of inquiry. During Colonel Higginson's absence Mrs. Higginson had moved to Newport, Rhode Island, and that pleasant town remained their home until her death in 1877. Higginson never returned to the ministry, but devoted himself to writing, turning out magazine articles on an immense variety of subjects from swimming to spiritualism, as well as a novel, short stories, book reviews and his well-known *Young Folks' History of the United States*. He concerned himself also with matters of local importance in Newport, and delivered public speeches and lectures in many places, carrying on meanwhile an active social life which his wife could share to only a limited degree.

The correspondence with Emily Dickinson was renewed and a number of poems were enclosed with her letters. Still plagued by the elusiveness of his correspondent, he challenged her to appear. Emily, lonely in the loss of her dog, Carlo, replied, "Whom my Dog understood could not elude others," yet she firmly resisted all his efforts to lure her into the world in which he moved. As early as 1866 she asked, "Might I entrust you as my Guest to the Amherst Inn?" But it was not until the summer of 1870 that a vacation trip to the White Mountains gave him the opportunity to plan his route by way of Amherst. The letters he wrote about her to

Mrs. Higginson preserve the record of this memorable experience. Most revealing of all, however, is a passage from the article already referred to, which he wrote for the *Atlantic Monthly* when the publication of the first series of her *Poems* had aroused public interest in her personality: "She was much too enigmatical a being for me to solve in an hour's interview, and an instinct told me that the slightest attempt to direct cross-examination would make her withdraw into her shell; I could only sit still and watch as one does in the woods; I must name my bird without a gun, as recommended by Emerson."

Unless one doubts the sincerity of Emily's expressions of feeling in her letters to friends, it is clear that she believed she had talked with a great man, whose authority she could rely on. Writing to him a month after his visit, she asked his forgiveness for her ignorance, and called herself his "obedient Child." Yet, in spite of Colonel Higginson's delicacy of feeling in treating her as one does a wild bird, the tone of her letter shows that they had not really found a common meeting ground. She continued to send him poems, sometimes in groups of four or five, and as late as 1873 they were sometimes accompanied by a small note begging for instruction. That she had profited not at all from the instruction she had received had nothing to do with the value of all he said, and the correspondence must be continued for its own sake. "That it is true, Master, is the Power of all you write," she said in 1876, in regard to a magazine article of his she had read.

Everything he wrote was of interest to her, and she read his books and the articles that appeared in magazines that came to the house. She treasured many of his phrases, and in one instance sent back to him a thought of his she had read fifteen years before as if it had been her own. In an article called "My Outdoor Study," published in the *Atlantic Monthly* for September 1861, he had said, "One can find summer in January by poring over the Latin catalogues of Massachusetts plants and animals in Hitchcock's reports." In a letter written in the winter of 1877, Emily wrote, "When Flowers annually died and I was a child, I used to read Dr. Hitchcock's Book on the Flowers of North America. This comforted their Absence — assuring me they lived." Emily's inaccuracy — for Dr. Hitchcock's study was confined to the flowers of his own state — adds more than it detracts from the impression of her high esteem for Colonel Higginson. In the same letter she quoted a sentence from the "Letter to a Young Contributor," citing it as her enduring authority for refusal to those who asked for her verses for publication: "Such being the majesty of the art you presume to practice, you can at least take time before dishonoring it."

After their meeting in 1870 the correspondence began to take on a more personal tone, and following the second visit in 1873 Emily began to include Mrs. Higginson through inquiry and occasional letters and poems, with small gifts of pressed flowers. During those years Mrs. Higginson, who seems to have been a life-long sufferer from arthritis, was becoming increasingly crippled, until in 1875 she was confined most of the time to a wheel chair.

Mary Channing Higginson was her husband's first cousin, and a sister of William Ellery Channing, the Concord poet.

She was several years older than her husband, to whom she had become engaged when he was a boy of nineteen. One feels that his choice may have been on the grounds of intellectual compatibility and family affection at a time when he was still emotionally immature, but the attachment survived through the four years of their engagement, and he gave her his tender devotion through all the years of her invalidism. A woman of marked intelligence and character, and, it was said, with gifts equal to her brother's, she might have taken a place of her own in some field of intellectual activity if it had not been for the serious handicap of poor health. As it was, the struggle to carry on daily living with the burden of constant pain limited her severely, but seems to have intensified her perceptions. She had the gift of pungent wit in her observations on persons and events, and could even see the humorous aspects of her own situation. She undoubtedly lightened the grimness of the circumstances for her husband as well as herself by her witty comments on people and books and the small happenings of daily life.

Colonel Higginson's letters to his sisters recount many of his wife's sayings, and she often added small penciled notes on the margin, giving in a few words a picture taken from her surroundings at the moment, or a comment on some topic of interest to them both. Characteristic of these is the following, dated May 17, 1874: "I am watching the opposite farmer who only works with a kitchen knife — which I approve — We must have faith in nature." The quality of this comment is so similar to Emily Dickinson's form of humor that, had the latter ever felt free to show that aspect of her mind to the

Higginsons, they might have found her less remote from normality than she appeared to them. Whether it was from awe or because the relation began with a single purpose, Emily never dropped her deferentially serious manner in writing to the man who, she said, had saved her life through his encouragement at a time of crisis. It is easy to see that her intensity might have been embarrassing, if it did not actually appear in bad taste, to a woman of Mrs. Higginson's type, and equally foreign to the nature of her husband.

Mrs. Higginson died in September 1877. Colonel Higginson wrote in his diary, "Who is taking care of her? is the cruel question that is never answered, when those we love are gone. With all Mary's strength she was such a child in her dependence on me and asked so often this year 'You'll stay by me, won't you?' yet she could not stay by me. It is hard to realize that her dependence ceased with the body." Emily wrote him four letters in close succession, expressing her sympathy in terms that suggest an intimacy he probably never felt. He could hardly have failed to be touched, however, and in his reply he seems to have hinted that he might go to see her. Several times in the ensuing months she wrote eagerly of her hope of seeing him, but he never visited her again, and his next trip to Amherst was to attend her funeral, nearly nine years later.

Colonel Higginson was soon able to take up his various interests, and as he was now free to travel, he visited Florida and then spent six months in Europe. After his return in the autumn of 1878, he became engaged to Miss Mary Thacher, whom he had known since she was a young girl. She was already the author of a little volume of pleasant essays called *Seashore and Prairie*, in one of which Higginson is mentioned as "the Professor." Later she published a children's story and two small volumes of verse. At the time of their marriage in February 1879, Colonel Higginson bought a house in Cambridge, and here they lived for the rest of his long life. This second marriage to a younger woman brought him a more normal family life than had been possible under the sad conditions of the first.

No one followed the course of this new phase with more sympathy than did Emily. Although fearful at first of intruding, she soon found occasions for letters. She continued to write to him through her last years, still signing herself "Your Scholar," and sending small gifts to his little girl. The new situation in his life must have put him in a different light for her, and the maturity of her own later years freed her to express herself in more simple human terms. Colonel Higginson noted the change himself, when writing his account of the correspondence in the *Atlantic Monthly* article, commenting on the more objective attitude she showed in a letter written in the summer of 1880, and concluding, "how close might have been her observation and sympathy, had her rare qualities taken a somewhat different channel." Her inner stress and intensity, however, were never lost, as is shown by the last words she ever wrote to him. Turning to him once more, less than a month before she died, she sent her final appeal, "Deity, does he live now? My friend, does he breathe?"

Thus ends the story of the strangely unequal friendship

which, in spite of its imbalance, held a place of great importance in the life of Emily Dickinson. Since only three of
Colonel Higginson's letters to her survive, it is necessary to
reconstruct much of what he said by reflection, as seen in her
replies. In view of the lack of direct evidence it is hardly fair
to place on his shoulders the sole responsibility for the fact
that during her lifetime only a handful of her verses appeared
in print, and none of those on her own initiative. Her own
inclination should carry its share, as an underlying reason
for her avoidance of publicity. Yet Higginson's influence was
without doubt the most important factor outside of herself.
A letter from a woman who met him at Newport in 1872
quotes him as saying of Emily Dickinson's poems, that they
"always reminded him of skeleton leaves, so pretty, but *too
delicate* — not strong enough to publish."

In one of his earliest letters Higginson advised Emily not
to publish. Her reply, "that [publication] being foreign to
my thought as Firmament to Fin," is divested of its absolute-
ness by the statement, "If fame belonged to me I could not
escape her," the truth of which has been proven. The poem
beginning

> Publication – is the Auction
> Of the Mind of Man –

often quoted to show her antipathy to seeing her verse in
print, ends:

> But reduce no Human Spirit
> To Disgrace of Price –

If this may be taken literally, it was the sale, not the circulation of poetry that she found most distasteful. A poem, after all, requires a reader for its fulfillment.

In her earliest phase as a poet Emily's friend Ben Newton had filled the place of reader and critic. Her brother Austin's wife, Susan Gilbert Dickinson, provided a ready audience close at hand, and a few other friends had been given an opportunity to read some of the verses. But, when Emily sent poems to the author of the "Letter to a Young Contributor," she could hardly have done so with a view to preserving them unread in a bureau drawer. If Higginson had perceived in them the work of an original genius who should be made known, it seems probable that her resistance to publicity would finally have been overcome. To her he represented the best the educated world could offer. If her poetry did not meet the world's requirements as he knew them, there was no need for her to seek elsewhere. She could be no one but herself, and she must therefore remain herself in private.

In a sense, however, she had her public in Higginson himself: the one reader outside the circle of her family and the few friends she had chosen from those whom family contacts had brought within her reach. From the beginning he received her letters and their enclosures with kindly courtesy, and as years went by with a warmer interest. His fine feeling is shown in his early recognition of his inability to effect any changes in her work without damaging what he called her "fine edge of thought." But he obviously could not classify it as poetry. In a letter he wrote after his second visit to her in December 1873, he referred to her verse as "the beautiful thoughts and words you have sent me." It seems to have remained in his mind, as in the minds of some of her other friends, as a personal form of expression, entirely removed from the world of published literature. Even after her death, when he was collaborating with Mrs. Todd in editing for publication the first series of her poems, he wrote to his sister that they were "very remarkable, though odd." Sad as it is that she never was to know her own power as reflected in the opinion of others, it may have been best that she was not subjected to the opposition or the neglect of a public that was not ready to receive her.

There is no likeness of the face of Emily Dickinson as a mature woman. Its absence denotes the privacy in which she lived. Some areas of her life can never be invaded, and to do so would be irrelevant to the main purpose of the biographer — to discover the factors, both outer and inner, that shaped the woman and the poet. The seeming contradiction between her seclusion and the vitality and depth of understanding in her poems is no contradiction, but a positive exponent of her power. One of the most personal of poets, and one of the most universal, in her narrow environment she focused all that she was upon each experience to extract its essence. The source of her power to transmute it into art was not disclosed, even to herself.

Best Things dwell out of Sight
The Pearl – the Just – Our Thought.

Most shun the Public Air
Legitimate, and Rare –

The Capsule of the Wind
The Capsule of the Mind

Exhibit here, as doth a Burr –
Germ's Germ be where?

Emily Dickinson

A NOTE ON SOURCES

The texts of all the Dickinson poems and letters are printed as a whole or in part as they appear in *The Poems of Emily Dickinson* (Cambridge, Mass., 1955) and *The Letters of Emily Dickinson* (Cambridge, Mass., 1958). Those that are covered by the Harvard copyright are reproduced through the courtesy of The President and Fellows of Harvard College.

Eighteen poems and excerpts from poems still in copyright under the control of Little, Brown & Company are reproduced with permission. One poem and excerpts from two others, as well as portions of seven letters still under copyright control by Houghton Mifflin Company, are reprinted with permission.

Sixteen poems and excerpts from four letters were first published in *Bolts of Melody* (New York, 1945), *Emily Dickinson: a Revelation* (New York, 1954), and *Emily Dickinson's Home* (New York, 1955), by Millicent Todd Bingham. They are reprinted here by permission of The President and Fellows of Harvard College and the Trustees of Amherst College.

The letters of Edward Dickinson to his wife and children, a letter from Judge Otis P. Lord to Lavinia Dickinson, and three letters of Thomas Wentworth Higginson to Emily Dickinson are among the Dickinson papers at Houghton Library, Harvard University. Excerpts from them are published with the permission of the Library. The letters of Samuel Bowles to Austin and Susan Dickinson are in the same collection. Excerpts from the diaries of Thomas Wentworth Higginson and his letters to his mother and sisters, also at Houghton Library, are used with the permission of the Library.

The letters of Thomas Wentworth Higginson to his wife, mentioned on page 189, are at the Boston Public Library.

An unidentified excerpt on page 194 is from a letter to Emily Fowler Ford from Lydia B. Torrey. It is among the Ford Papers at the New York Public Library, and is printed with the permission of the Library.

A NOTE ON SOURCES

Heman Humphrey's *Revival Conversations*, quoted on page 17, was published in Boston in 1844.

George F. Whicher's *This Was a Poet*, mentioned on page 28, was published by Charles Scribner's Sons, New York and London, 1939.

A quotation from Thomas H. Johnson on page 89 is from his book, *Emily Dickinson: An Interpretive Biography* (Cambridge, Mass., 1955).

A quotation from Solomon Bulkley Griffin on page 116 is from his book, *People and Politics, Observed by a Massachusetts Editor* (Boston, 1923).

Josiah Gilbert Holland by Mrs. H. M. Plunkett, mentioned on page 119, was published by Charles Scribners Sons in 1894.

The review by James Russell Lowell of J. G. Holland's *Bitter-Sweet*, mentioned on page 127, appeared in the *Atlantic Monthly*, May 1859.

The Life and Times of Samuel Bowles by George S. Merriam, mentioned on page 177, was published by the Century Company, 1885.

Thomas Wentworth Higginson's article "Emily Dickinson's Letters," quoted on page 189, appeared in the *Atlantic Monthly*, October 1891.

INDEX OF POEMS

INDEX OF POEMS

INDEX

INDEX

INDEX